Lost for
words

Lost for
words

**For all who think
evangelism
is not for them**

JAMES LAWRENCE

Text copyright © James Lawrence 1999

The author asserts the moral right
to be identified as the author of this work

Published by
The Bible Reading Fellowship
Peter's Way, Sandy Lane West
Oxford OX4 6HG
ISBN 1 84101 096 0

First published 1999
1 3 5 7 9 10 8 6 4 2

Acknowledgments

Scripture quotations are taken from the *Holy Bible, New International Version*, copyright © 1973, 1978, 1984 by International Bible Society. Used by permission of Hodder & Stoughton Limited. All rights reserved. 'NIV' is a registered trademark of International Bible Society. UK trademark number 1448790.

A catalogue record for this book is available from the British Library

Printed and bound in Great Britain by
Omnia Books Limited, Glasgow

For
Sophie
William
and **Toby**

Acknowledgments

I find myself 'lost for words' simply because I don't know where to start. So many people have invested so much to make this book a reality. Bar Hill Church where much of this material first started its tentative journey. Richard Zair, Anne Hibbert, Roger Murphy, Jane Wigman, Carol Street and Nadia Evans at CPAS who have shaped the material. Jacky Bowers, Mark Brown, Tim Hollingdale, David Male who have patiently read it and offered their insights. Rory Keegan who has been a constant inspiration to work hard at every sentence. Naomi Starkey at BRF for waiting patiently and giving such helpful advice. Countless others who have taught me about evangelism. Thank you. Above all, thank you to David and Kenneth who brought me to faith. There is no greater gift.

Contents

Foreword

How do you help 'ordinary' Christians to share their faith effectively? There is no shortage of books and manuals on that topic, so why another? One of the crucial lessons that we have learned in *Springboard* is that 'ordinary' people do it best. That is not to discount the particular gifts of those called to be evangelists—far from it. But it is to recognize that most of those who come new into Christian discipleship do so through the everyday life and witness of friends and not through the visiting celebrity. Indeed, many of us find that we are de-skilled and disempowered by the superstars. They make it look so easy. So, by implication, we who make heavy weather of it are less usable by God.

For the last few years, James Lawrence has been an invaluable part-time member of the *Springboard* core team. He has enabled hundreds of folk to examine their faith, to sharpen up what they believe and to communicate it with a new confidence. Ironically, James himself could be seen as a potential superstar, but he has developed such an insight into the fears and struggles of the average churchgoer that what he has to offer is not seen as threatening. On the contrary, it is the apparent ordinariness of his illustrations and the clear simplicity of his presentation that makes him so accessible. The characters you will meet in these pages are characters that you will already know.

The substance of this book is well thought out but it is certainly not a merely cerebral exercise. The material has been road-tested and refined by use. It is now presented as a useful resource to a church approaching the end of the Decade of Evangelism—a church which, I pray, is gearing itself up for the next stage of proclaiming Christ afresh to the next generation.

+ *Colin Coventry*
Co-chair of Springboard, *the Archbishops' Initiative for Evangelism*

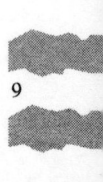

Sunday morning at church

'...and how can they hear if no one tells them?' Simon closes the Bible. 'Here ends the reading.'

Dorothy shuffles in her seat. She hopes the sermon won't be too long this morning, as she can't remember if she turned the oven on for the Sunday roast.

Geoff is, as always, sitting on his own.

Mary breathes a sigh of relief. 'A few moments of peace and quiet now that the kids have gone to Sunday school. It would be so much easier if Bob came to church as well.'

Roger and Alison hold each other's hands firmly. 'It's been seven months now.'

Injit struggles to focus his mind. 'Work has been unbelievably busy this quarter, and with that deadline pressing for Thursday...'

Tom smiles at Simon as he walks back to his seat. 'It's so good to see him involved after all these years.'

As he sits down, Simon's relief is tangible. 'Thank goodness I didn't stumble over the words.'

Naomi stands to preach. 'Thank you, Simon. Our subject this morning is evangelism. We'll be considering the passage from Romans which Simon has just read. Let's bow our heads to pray.'

Dorothy sneaks a quick look at her watch as she closes her eyes. 'Oh dear, I'm sure she'll go on. She loves talking about evangelism.'

'Heavenly Father, thank you...'

Geoff buries his head in his hands. 'Yes, thank you for so

much, but I wish you'd made me more able to talk to people. Then I could be more use for you, Lord.'

'...*that you have shown yourself to us.*'

Mary's heart sinks. 'I'm such a failure when it comes to this evangelism. I can't even talk to my husband about it. Every time I try, we end up in a row. It's not any easier with my friends.'

'*Thank you that you love us and long for us to share our faith.*'

Alison's grip tightens on Roger's hand. 'Love us, love us. So why did you let it happen? A week, that's all. Everything is such a struggle at the moment. What have I got to share?'

'*Please help us to speak to our friends...*'

Injit hurriedly scribbles down a note on the back of the notice sheet, hoping no one will spot him. 'Friends, I'd love to have some friends. There simply isn't time, what with work and the family.'

'...*about the good news...*'

Tom smiles again. 'Twenty years since I first heard that good news.'

'...*so they too may become Christians.*'

Simon's frown deepens. 'It would be nice to have a few more in church on Sundays but I can't see what I can do. I'm so new myself.'

'*Amen.*'

Their response is automatic: 'Amen.'

Introduction—
the dreaded E-word

Evangelism. It's an emotive word. Mention it and you are bound to get a reaction. Ideas, images, feelings, concerns, experiences all bubble to the surface. That dreaded evangelism word. Go on, be honest—how would *your* church react this Sunday if the sermon were on evangelism?

I imagine your church's reaction would be similar to that of Naomi's congregation. For some, images of door-knocking, Billy Graham, televangelists, soap boxes, crusades, football stadiums, tents, and singing choirs. For some, apprehension, embarrassment and little interest. For some, fear, disillusionment, concern and guilt. For some, excitement, interest and a longing to be involved. No wonder a sermon on evangelism is likely to cause a stir.

And how would *you* respond? Are you thrilled by the word? Do you find it easy to talk about your faith? If so, great. If, however, you find yourself tongue-tied, lost for words, struggling with fear, uncertain whether you want to have anything to do with it, then please read on. This book is written for people just like you. It's my passionate conviction that the coal-face of evangelism is ordinary Christian people in their everyday lives. Christians like Dorothy, Geoff, Mary, Roger, Alison, Injit, Tom and Simon. Christians like you and me. People with fears, hopes, ideas, concerns and un-certainties that need exploring. This book is not for expert evangelists, it is for all who are prepared to explore what their role may be in God's ongoing work of evangelism.

When I speak about evangelism in this book, I am not referring to special events, particular people or specific activities, good as these may be. Instead, I want to consider everyday life. In this context I define evangelism as 'co-operating with God in helping people discover and respond to the good news about Jesus, through prayer, lifestyle, conversation and concern'. This is primarily God's work, not ours. He invites us to co-operate with him.

In particular, we are going to focus on talking about our faith in a way that is *relaxed*, *natural* and *helpful*. It's not something that many of us find easy, yet God has chosen to use people like us in the way he communicates his good news to others.

As I write this, we are approaching Christmas and the words to the shepherds in the field have gripped me again: 'Do not be afraid. I bring you good news of great joy that will be for all the people' (Luke 2:10). We'll be considering the 'good news of great joy' later in the book. We'll also be identifying our fears that hold us back from exploring our faith with others, but it's the words 'for all people' that have found their mark in my heart.

'All people.' That means Simon who lives along my road, Jo whom I play squash with, John the guy at work, Peter our postman, Sally and Keith my friends from long ago, our two children, Nick and Sue down at the playschool, Mary the girl I met at the New Year party, Tony that boy I never got on with at school, and many others I'm in contact with as life goes on. 'All people.' Who does it mean for you? Who are the people you are in regular contact with?

You and I may be the only Christians these people know, and God longs to use us to help them discover the one who is at the heart of the good news of great joy—to use us just as we are, to use us right now. You may like to join with me in a simple prayer before we go any further.

A prayer
Lord, here I am.
Please help me to know you,
to love people,
and to discover my role in evangelism. Amen

Sunday at church: the sermon

Simon missed the opening sentences of the sermon. It was the first time he'd done the reading. 'Not so bad after all. Now, what was it all about?

Naomi seemed to be looking his way. 'So often, we don't speak about our faith because of fear...'

'How does she know? I'm sure people at work will make fun of me if they find out I've become a Christian. Anyway, I don't want to come across as some sort of Bible basher—they have enough of that from Angie in Sales. I'm sure it's better to keep it to myself until I know a bit more about it, then I might be able to answer some of those difficult questions.'

'Some of us here may already have switched off,' Naomi continued. 'We have tried to talk about our faith and it all went horribly wrong. Please switch back on...'

Mary's mind was wandering. 'There was that time when I tried to talk to my brother about Jesus. Now that was a disaster, and when I got angry with him he simply looked at me and said, "Call yourself a Christian?" Friends aren't any easier. I get so wound up about it that I can hardly string two words together and I make a complete fool of myself. I'm just no good at this evangelism thing... What was that about switching back on...?'

Dorothy sneaked another look at her watch. Naomi was in full flow. Lunch was going to be very late.

Naomi paused and smiled. 'Look at Billy Graham. He is one of the most famous people in the world today...'

Dorothy had guessed he'd be mentioned. 'He's great, that Billy Graham, I remember going to Haringay myself when I was a teenager. In some ways, Tom and Naomi remind me of him. They seem to have the gift of the gab.'

Anyone sitting near Geoff would have seen him smile. He enjoyed it when Naomi preached. She was so good at putting things clearly. She continued, 'I was standing at the bus stop the other day, and as usual the bus was delayed. There were half a dozen of us waiting so I started chatting to a couple of them next to me, and before I knew it we were talking about Jesus...'

'If only I could be like Naomi,' Geoff mused. 'She is so natural when talking to people and never seems lost for words. I couldn't do that, talk to a crowd of strangers. Evangelism would be so much easier if I was an extrovert like Naomi rather than the introvert I am.'

'She was very aggressive when we first started talking,' said Naomi. 'No, she didn't believe in God. No, she didn't think Jesus was that important. No, she didn't find my experiences convincing, they were just *my* experiences. But as we talked I shared the gospel with her...'

Holding Alison's hand, Roger pondered his ten years as a Christian. 'I rarely ever talk to anyone about Jesus, let alone a complete stranger. There was Chris at work, but all I did was suggest he might like to try an Alpha course.'

Injit made further frantic scribbles on the notice sheet. In between, he caught patches of Naomi's sermon.

'Thankfully, we have moved on from those days when evangelism was about the number of scalps you could notch up on your belt. Of course, I exaggerate, but there were some rather extreme ideas about. We now recognize it's about friendship evangelism...'

'There's that word again. I'm up to my eyes at work, struggling to keep my job. The commuting is exhausting and I don't have enough time to spend with family as it is. Of the few friends I have, one has become a Christian and the other two have moved away. I just don't have time to make any more friends. I feel so pathetic. I know it's important, Lord, but I could do without any more time commitments at the moment. Do you mind if I pass on this one?'

A tear trickled down Roger's cheek despite his determination to get through the service without weeping. Alison looked away to pull herself together, half hearing Naomi's voice. 'When our faith means so much to us...' she continued.

'That's just the point. I'm not sure whether it does any more. It has been such a desperate time. What have I got to share? Confusion, questions, pain. Oh Lord...'

It was twenty-four minutes before Naomi uttered her final 'Amen'. Simon timed it.

Chapter 1

Let's be honest...

How would you respond to Naomi's sermon on evangelism—honestly?

Honesty is a great virtue, but sadly it's not always found in church circles, especially when we talk about evangelism. We nod our heads approvingly. Outwardly we agree, inwardly we groan. Few dare to break the code of silence. The truth may be out there, but we rarely discover it. Who dares to state honestly what they really think or feel about evangelism?

A few months ago, I was leading a church weekend away on the theme of evangelism. In the first session I asked the participants to discuss this question in pairs: 'What feelings or thoughts does the word "evangelism" produce in you?' I invited them to be honest. The conversation was animated. After a few minutes I asked them to call out some of their feelings and thoughts and recorded them on a flip-chart. As they listened to each other's honest reactions, there was a tangible sense of relief. One person expressed it well. She exclaimed, 'But I thought I was the only one who struggled with evangelism.'

She certainly isn't. Every time I've done this exercise, the vast majority of the feelings and thoughts expressed are negative. The same issues crop up again and again. Here are some of the most common ones:

- Fear and embarrassment
- Inadequacy and failure
- Fine for other people to do, but not for me
- It's not my gift
- Don't know what to say

- Lack of friends who aren't Christians
- Struggling with faith

Let's be honest... Any of these ring bells? They certainly do in Naomi's congregation, and I imagine they probably do in our own churches. If we are to make progress we need to face up to these struggles, openly admit our difficulties and help each other through them. Let's explore a few of them through people within Naomi's congregation.

Simon: 'I'm frightened of how people will respond'

Simon is really concerned about how people will respond. He is struggling with fear. What will his workmates say when they find out he's a Christian? How will he answer their questions? Fear takes many forms, but the fears people talk about most often are fear of ridicule, fear of rejection, fear of not knowing what to say, and fear of putting someone off. Fear is crippling. It spreads slowly, thriving when we don't attend to it. Even when we do face up to our fear and try to deal with it, it has an alarming capacity to grow back.

Recently we decided to remove an ivy from the front of our house. The roots were damaging the foundations and the foliage was eating into the brickwork. It had even managed to entwine itself around the rafters. As ever with these household chores, I put it off for more months than I care to remember. When eventually we could no longer open our son's bedroom window, we decided to take action. It took an age to pull the ivy off the brickwork, releasing one branch after another. By the time we'd finished, it was dark, and there was no time to tackle the main stem and roots. To my embarrassment, if you call at our home today you will see it still firmly stuck in the soil at the front of the house. And to my annoyance, it is growing all over again.

Fear is not unlike my ivy. It entangles itself around the foundations and damages the fabric of our lives. One quick tug is not enough to shift it. It takes concerted effort over a long period of time. But we need to start somewhere, releasing one branch at a time and eventually digging out the root. So what can we do?

Identify our fears

What are our specific fears about evangelism? If we don't identify the problem, we are unlikely to tackle it. Like the ivy, it may have been around a long time, and we've got so used to it that we don't easily see the damage it is doing.

Talk about our fears

We are not alone in struggling with fear. All it takes is one person being open and honest and then others are encouraged to be honest as well. We are far more likely to tackle our fears when we tackle them together. It just takes someone to start.

Ask God for help

As with that ivy, it can take time to remove fear. Some aspects we may struggle with for the rest of our lives, but God's love gives us courage to take the next step despite our fears. God's love refocuses us away from our feelings to the needs of others. God's love assures us that he is always with us. The master gardener is at work, pruning, digging, clearing, so that the fabric and foundation of our lives may be released from fear. Let's ask for God's help.

It may also be helpful to recognize that some of our fears can lead to appropriate sensitivity in relationships. If we fear hurting someone's feelings or damaging our friendship with them, we'll be more likely to approach them in a loving way. There is a thin dividing line between appropriate concern and inappropriate fear.

Co-operating with God in evangelism requires honesty, facing our fears, and loving people enough to proceed in the face of fear.

Mary: 'I've tried, and made such a mess'

Would you like to join a club? I'm afraid the membership is hardly exclusive, but you are more than welcome to join. It's for all those who suffer from the 'if-only' syndrome. Mary is a member. She looks back at her attempts to talk about her faith and remembers the mess she's made. If only I'd said that… if only I hadn't said… if only I'd kept my mouth closed… if only I'd opened my mouth and said something… if only I hadn't got into that argument… if only I'd listened more carefully… and so it goes on. I'm a fully paid-up lifetime member of this club. Rarely a conversation goes by about Christianity when I don't end up thinking 'If only…'

I remember one of my earliest attempts at talking about my faith. The guy was a bit of a hard nut to crack, but of course there was no one better than me to have a go. Five minutes into the discussion, I was suddenly left standing on my own. 'What's got into him?' I thought. 'Must be conviction,' I surmised. Some minutes later, a mutual friend came up and told me what had got into him. 'He was so annoyed by your arrogance, he wanted to hit you.' Did I have some lessons to learn!

How do we handle negative past experiences?

Honest reflection

It is worth reflecting on what we said and how we said it, but beware—we are not always the best ones to judge a situation. My initial reflection on the incident above was mistaken. I thought it was his problem. It wasn't. It was my insensitive approach. Reflecting with someone else helped me to see my insensitivity and arrogance. I learnt from the experience. I needed to apologize to him. It wasn't the last time I've needed to apologize, either.

Alternatively, someone else can encourage us. Often I think I've made a terrible mess. Talking to someone else helps me see things more accurately: it may not be as bad as I initially thought. Together we can work out ways to handle the situation better next time.

Don't despair

Whatever else happens, let's not despair. Don't ever think God can't or won't use us. Don't be tempted to shy away from having another go. God wants to use us. If, like me, you have had your fair share of 'if only...' situations, remember that God is the one who can take our fumbling attempts and use them for his purposes. God has been in the business a very long time. Thankfully, he is rather good at it.

Evangelism involves having a go, making mistakes, learning through reflection, and trusting that God can still use us.

Dorothy: 'It's not my thing— I'll leave it to the experts'

When we speak of the E-word, we need to recognize that there are actually two E-words. They are closely related: evangelism and evangelist. In some people's minds they are the same. That's why, for many, their expectations about evangelism are fuelled by their experience of evangelists. Such experiences may have been positive, in which case we will probably be in awe of those who seem to find talking about the faith so easy. Some experiences may have been negative, in which case we are unlikely to want to have anything to do with evangelism. Dorothy loves Billy Graham, and is delighted Naomi is so excited about evangelism, but when she compares herself to them she decides it's not her thing. She could never speak to thousands. She'll leave it up to them.

God has gifted some to be the evangelists, but that doesn't exclude us from playing our part in evangelism. In the same way, God gifts some to be intercessors but we are all called to play our part in intercession; some are gifted as leaders of worship but we are all called to worship. Playing our part does *not* involve becoming a Billy Graham clone. God does not expect us to preach to thousands, nor does he necessarily expect us to go door-knocking, standing on soap boxes or talking to complete strangers.

Good as these things may be, everyday evangelism does not focus on them. Rather, its focus is on ordinary Christian people in contact with ordinary people who aren't Christians in the course of their everyday lives.

Decades ago, William Temple, then Archbishop of Canterbury, put it like this:

The evangelization of England is a work that cannot be done by the clergy alone; it can only be done to a very small extent by the clergy at all. There can be no widespread evangelization of England unless the work is undertaken by the lay people of the church… The main duty of the clergy must be to train the lay members of their congregations in their work of witness.

We need our Billy Grahams, Toms, Naomis and whoever the gifted evangelists are in our church, but please don't think we have to be like them, or that evangelism is to be left to the evangelists—or our minister, for that matter.

Evangelism involves us all.

Geoff: 'I'm rather shy'

I visited a vicar last week, and we talked about evangelism. At one point he said, 'Of course, I am the world's worst evangelist.' It soon became clear why he felt this way. He was living under the mistaken assumption that if he were extrovert by character he would somehow be far more useful for evangelism. Geoff thinks the same. He's an introvert by nature, finds crowds of people difficult, and prefers being with one or two people he knows well. He looks at extroverts and thinks he's got to become more like them if he is to be involved with evangelism.

Geoff doesn't need a personality transplant. Nor do we. God wants to use us just as we are. God uses all personality types to reach all personality types. Are we clear thinkers? God wants to use us. Do we 'feel' our way to decisions? God wants to use us. Are we cool and logical? God wants to use us. Are we intuitive types? God wants to use us. Are we passionate enthusiasts? God wants to use us. Are we quiet and reflective? God wants to use us. Are we outward-focused, 'go get it' characters? God wants to use us. Are we natural talkers? God wants to use us. Are we shy? God wants to use us. Are we…?

Evangelism involves being who we are.

Roger: 'It rarely happens to me'

Roger is concerned. People don't come up to him at work and ask him about his faith. In fact, no one has even asked him why he behaves differently from others. He suspects he's never engaged in 'proper evangelism' because he's never seen a person become a Christian as a result of his efforts. And that is what it is all about… isn't it? Well… yes, and no. Yes, we long for people to become Christians. But no, it will not be the regular experience of the majority of Christians directly to help a person put their faith in Christ, to be there as they make their commitment. Some would argue that it should be, that we just don't have enough faith, or aren't expectant enough, or haven't received the right training. I'm not so sure, for two reasons.

Reason one: Evangelism is a body ministry

We are all called to play our part in evangelism, but each part differs. Over the last few years, I've struggled with a question: what are appropriate evangelistic expectations for every Christian? One thing has become clear—not to expect too much too soon of too many.

When I first became a minister of a church, I led two evangelism training courses. The course material was well produced and twenty people signed up enthusiastically. They weren't evangelists but were keen to learn more about evangelism. After five or six

weeks we began to run into problems. Not being sure what to do, I simply pressed on. Six months after the course finished, I gently enquired how things were going. The responses were illuminating. Here was the problem.

The expectations set by the course were exciting—that we would regularly lead people to faith in Christ, yet six months later the reality of everyday experience struck. What the course members were led to expect from the course didn't become reality in their lives. Quickly, they either became disillusioned or felt guilty. Disillusioned because it didn't happen in the way they expected and guilty because they thought they were somehow to blame.

The real problem was not with the participants but with the way the course set up unhelpful and unrealistic expectations. All too often, this happens because those who are evangelists, or who have been involved in evangelism for a long time, write evangelism courses. In their excitement they long for others to share their experience, and through a course they project their gifts and experiences on to others. But we are all different. Some people may never pray a prayer of commitment with an individual. That doesn't mean they aren't involved in evangelism. It just means that evangelism is a body ministry where we all have different parts to play, where we all need one another.

Some are excellent at serving people through loving acts; others are great at making people feel welcome. Some are good at tackling life issues creatively from a Christian perspective; others are superb at introducing Jesus into conversations in a relaxed way. Some can argue detailed theological points; others are good at inviting people to events. Some, normally the evangelists amongst us, are good at helping people to take the first step of faith; others are good at caring for them when they are Christians. No one person is likely to be good at all of the above. We need one another.

Listening to those who regularly lead people to commitment to Christ is thrilling. Let's rejoice with them and thank God for the gift they have. It is equally significant to hear of Roger inviting Chris to an Alpha course, or Sandra praying with Kim about her forthcoming operation, or Mike bringing Sam along to church one Sunday. We all have our part to play in the body ministry of evangelism—but each part is different.

Reason two: Evangelism is as much about process as crisis

Some people come to faith in Christ through a sudden experience, but most do not. It can happen like that, it does happen like that, but it is not the norm. People more often come through a process that takes some time. John Finney's research at the start of the Decade of Evangelism identified that twenty to thirty per cent of those interviewed described their coming to faith as a sudden event, and seventy to eighty per cent as a process over time. My own questioning of many Christians over the years backs this up. Yet I think it helps to recognize that there is a danger of caricaturing the process/crisis issue. In reality, the majority of people who talk of a process can identify significant moments along the way. Those people who talk of a dramatic event often recognize the way God was at work in their lives before the event.

If coming to faith is seen as a process, a journey, people will need all sorts of help along the way. God simply asks us to accompany people on the next step of their journey. That may be the stirring of interest in Christianity, it may be the desire to find out more, it may be to deal with particular questions, it may be the need to feel they belong.

Mandy used to live next door. One frosty evening I returned from church and we started to chat over the fence. She asked me where I'd been, and I explained. I asked her if she had ever been to church, and she mentioned that she used to go as a child but gave up when she left home. I asked her why, and she said, 'I couldn't see its relevance to my life.' I sympathized. My experience of church as a teenager hadn't been particularly helpful either, but I went on to say, 'It made a huge difference when I realized that

Christianity wasn't primarily about church-going but knowing God in a life-transforming way.' We spent a further ten minutes talking before the cold got to both of us and we retreated to our own homes.

I wish I could say she was converted on the spot, or even the next day. She wasn't. Within four weeks she had moved—not, I hope, as a result of our conversation! I am no longer in touch with Mandy, but I hope it helped her take one further step along the path to faith in Christ. Who knows, you might be the next person God wants to use to help her on the journey.

Evangelism involves faithfulness to the opportunity God gives us to accompany someone on the next step of the journey to faith.

Injit: 'I haven't time for friends who aren't Christians'

Injit feels guilty and excluded. Guilty because he thinks he should be doing something about it, excluded because he can't see where he can find the time for friendship evangelism. I've come across many 'Injits' in the church. His situation raises a number of issues.

Over-busy Christians

One of the great problems is the hyperactive church that breeds the ghetto Christian who never has time to do anything outside the church. Churches, and individual Christians within them, need to take a serious look at diaries and programmes to identify the over-committed and over-busy. Those in greatest danger are often the paid church leaders. When I worked as a minister of a church, I discovered how easy it is to be so caught up with church work that there is no time for being with those who aren't yet Christians. As we are called to love our neighbours, so our churches need to help us with this, and I as a church leader needed to set an example. It was a great challenge to me to ask myself how much time I spent with people who weren't yet Christians.

Friendship evangelism

The term 'friendship evangelism' isn't always helpful. I recognize the reason for this emphasis—to build friendships as the basis for talking about matters of faith rather than the 'hit 'em quick' mentality—but I think it leads to confusion.

People define the word 'friend' in so many different ways. For some, a person they have just met is 'a friend'. For others, someone only becomes 'a friend' after many years of close contact. Christians in both these positions may be in regular contact with people who aren't Christians, and use the phrase 'friendship evangelism', but only one of them readily identifies someone they know. That's why in this book we will talk about 'contacts'. It may be rather a 'cold' phrase, but nearly every Christian is in regular face-to-face *contact* with people who aren't Christians—colleagues at work, neighbours, people we meet through interests or sports, or acquaintances.

Injit's situation raises another issue concerning 'friendship evangelism'. One of his friends has become a Christian, and the two others have moved out of the area. Naturally he doesn't want to ditch his existing friend in favour of someone else, and there is a limit to the amount of time he has. Injit also finds the idea of 'making friends' with an ulterior motive in mind—even if it is a good one—slightly uncomfortable.

The emphasis of this book is on 'relational' evangelism: not so much sharing our faith with 'friends', but sharing our faith with people we know in a friendly way.

'Friends and family'—the hardest people to talk to

Friends are often the hardest people to start with. For British Telecom, the phrase 'friends and family' may have a warm, comforting ring to it, but in evangelism the phrase 'friends and family' is far from a warm and comforting thought. Why do we struggle with those closest to us? Because they know us so well and because we have everything to lose. I find great encouragement in

seeing that the two groups of people Jesus had the most difficulty with were his family and close friends (see Mark 3:20–21; 6:1–6). We'll explore this issue further in Chapter 9.

Injit is in daily contact with people who aren't yet Christians. These are the people God wants him to be concerned for and pray for. Who are our daily contacts?

Evangelism involves starting with those we already relate to.

Alison: 'I'm struggling with my own faith'

Churches are full of people like Alison and Roger—people struggling with their faith. The reasons differ, but the reality is the same. When we feel distant from God or full of doubts ourselves, what possible use can we be?

In our own eyes we seem useless, but that doesn't mean God can't use us. For those in pain, for those with doubts, for those with questions, God is still able to work in us and through us. I think of a friend whose son died at seventeen, a colleague who experienced depression, a church member who struggled with doubts. Each of them found faith hard, yet God didn't give up on them. He has used those experiences for his purposes.

Of course, that is easier to say when looking back on past times of difficulty; it is harder to believe if we are actually living with difficulties at this moment. Yet so many people do speak of the reality of God's strength in their weakness. Incredible as it seems, he can use us even when we are falling apart, hurting or full of questions.

Evangelism involves trusting God, even in the dark places.

Face the struggle

Whatever we struggle with, whether it is one of the things listed above or something not mentioned, let's offer it to God and ask for his help. Let's be honest with other Christians and explore the issues with them. Let's determine to take a step forward, and not be held back.

- Evangelism involves being honest, facing our fear, and loving people enough to proceed despite them.
- Evangelism involves having a go, making mistakes, learning through reflection, and trusting that God still uses us.
- Evangelism involves us all.
- Evangelism involves being who we are.
- Evangelism involves being faithful to the opportunities God gives us to accompany people on the next step of the journey to faith.
- Evangelism involves starting with those we already know.
- Evangelism involves trusting God.

My son, William, loves Postman Pat. One of his favourite episodes is when a landslide blocks the road. He loves watching as Pat's friends try to get through in their old tractor. He knows they are not going to make it, but he's learnt what will get through: a tractor with a bulldozer blade. The blockage isn't completely cleared, but a path is made just wide enough for them to squeeze through. As they drive through, William whoops and cheers.

God may not completely clear the path, but he does want to create a gap wide enough for us to proceed. Whatever our struggle, whatever has blocked our involvement with evangelism in the past, God has the right way to deal with it. Let's ask him to have a go. Then let's take a step forward, and listen for the whoops and cheers of the angels.

To consider

Take a few moments to review the list of struggles. Which do you most closely identify with? Offer it to God in prayer, asking for his help, and if you have a Christian friend who would be sympathetic, talk to them about it as well.

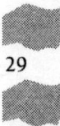

A prayer
Heavenly Father, my greatest blockage is ....
Please help me to face it honestly.
Give me the faith to trust you,
and the courage to move on. Amen.

Sunday: Dorothy, after church

'Two coffees, please.'

Dorothy poured out the coffee and, with her customary smile, handed it to Injit.

'See you at home-group on Wednesday,' she said.

'I'm not sure,' Injit replied hesitantly. 'Things are a little tight at work at the moment. I hope to make it.'

'Poor man,' she thought as he took the coffee off to his wife. 'He looks so tired.' She was washing up when Tom popped his head round the door.

'Need a hand?'

'That would be kind; I'm in a bit of a hurry because I think I forgot to put the roast on—old age, you know! I've got my daughter and her family coming for lunch.'

Tom smiled. 'So what did you make of the sermon this morning?'

'Well, if I'm honest, I was struggling a bit. It all seems so easy for people like you and Naomi. You have the gift of the gab. I never know where to start. I don't have many close friends outside the church, and those I do know... I often wonder what I can do. It's so much easier not to bother!'

Tom picked up another cup. 'I know what you mean. It can be quite a struggle. I wonder what the others in the home-group think about it all.'

'Why don't we talk about it on Wednesday night?' replied Dorothy, hanging up the dishcloth. 'I'm sure I am not the only one who finds evangelism hard.'

'That's a great idea. We can take the first part of the evening and find out what the others think, especially as

Naomi is planning to take the next three Sundays to focus on evangelism.'

On her way home, Dorothy bumped into her neighbour.

'Good morning, Brian, how are things?'

'Oh, Dorothy, sorry, must rush, my daughter has just been taken into hospital with a burst appendix. Ruth has gone to see her and I'm off to help look after the kids.'

Before she could respond, he was in the car and off down the street. 'Poor man. I wonder if there is anything that I could do to help.'

Chapter 2

It all started with a prayer

Dorothy is concerned. 'I'm not sure where to start… It's so much easier not to bother.' And she's right. It *is* easier not to bother with helping others discover the good news about Jesus. Even if we have identified some of the potential blockages, even if we have seen God clear a path through them, why is it that many of us still don't feel any great sense of need or urgency to press on down the evangelism route? In a word, *motivation*. All the circumstances can be right, but if I'm not motivated to do something I'm unlikely to do it.

Leighton Ford, in his excellent book *The Power of Story* (NavPress, 1994), identifies various reasons for being involved in evangelism, and concludes, 'I would suggest to you that the purest motivation of all for evangelism is vision… Vision means to see the world, and all the people in it, as God the Father sees them' (p. 79). This is the internal motivation for the Christian—to be so affected by God's vision for the world that it changes our character and inspires us to play our part in helping other people discover the good news about Jesus.

How does this happen? How do we see the world as God sees it? How do our hearts begin to beat in time with God's heart? How are our lives transformed so that we are more like Christ in our attitudes and actions each day? One of the early Christians gives us a clue as he writes to the church in Colossae: prayer.

'Devote yourselves to prayer,' Paul writes in Colossians 4:2. Here is the place to start. It is through prayer that God changes us, helping us to see things as he sees them. It is through prayer that God, in some mysterious way, works in his world. It is through prayer that we become more like Jesus, and his concerns become

our concerns, his attitudes our attitudes, his activity our activity. This is something all Christian people can be involved in, no matter what their circumstances, gifts or personality. Dorothy can pray. So can we, however falteringly.

How is our prayer life?

Prayer is another one of those things it's easy to feel guilty about, and I find that the greatest temptation with regard to prayer is to give up. Two consistent themes seem to emerge from the many books that are written on prayer today. First, pray as you can, not as you can't. Whatever you are able to do, do it. If that means saying the Lord's Prayer each morning when you wake up, then start there. But here's the second thing. The only way to learn how to pray is to pray. Books can guide us, but we still need to pray. This isn't a book primarily about prayer, but starting somewhere is better than doing nothing. Although it may seem a bit odd to start by focusing our prayers on helping others come to faith, we may find there is no better place to begin. What clues has Paul got to offer us?

Clue one: Keep on praying

Paul urges us, 'Devote yourselves to prayer' (Colossians 4:2). The word he uses for 'devote' loses some of its punch in this translation. It means keep on praying no matter what, don't give up. Why is Paul so emphatic about the priority of prayer? Because he knows prayer changes us and changes those we pray for. Time spent with God forms us. It forms our thinking, our actions, our feelings, our perspectives and priorities. Time spent with God changes us so that we reflect more and more the character and priorities of Jesus. I believe Paul knew what a struggle it was to share the faith, even to want to share the faith. He also knew that the key to finding a way forward is prayer. Motivation comes through a mindset and Paul is urging us to develop the mind of Christ through prayer.

Clue two: Focus your prayers through watchfulness

'Devote yourselves to prayer, *being watchful*' (Colossians 4:2). Does that mean keeping our eyes open?

I was in a prayer meeting with a dozen or so people I hadn't met before. We'd spoken about a number of things and decided it would be good to pray before our time ran out. When we finished, one man said, 'Why do you do that?' There was a circle of blank faces. None of us was quite sure what on earth he was on about. Eventually someone piped up, 'Do what?' 'Bury your head in your hands when you pray,' he responded. He went on, 'I am a Messianic Jew. We Jews know the importance of watchfulness in our praying. We look up and keep our eyes open. There are so many things around us that can prompt us to pray.'

I realize he was stressing a point. Of course we can pray with our eyes closed and still allow our mind's eye to prompt us in our praying, yet I find it helpful to develop what I call responsive praying, allowing what I see to inspire and inform my prayers.

I am often asked, 'But who should I pray for?' 'Be watchful' is my response. Dorothy isn't sure who to pray for, yet day by day she is in contact with a lot of people. Here are the people she can begin to serve through prayer. There's Jo at the club, having a hard time at the moment. Maggie along the street whose four-year-old is sleeping so badly. Neal at the corner shop, burgled for the fourth time in six months. Sanjit and Isher next door, about to go off on holiday. Brian and Ruth whose daughter has just been rushed into hospital. All these are people Dorothy is in contact with, all of them with particular things she could pray for.

What about us? Who are we in regular contact with, who isn't yet a Christian? How could 'being watchful' lead us in our prayers for them? As Nick Pollard says in *Evangelism Made Slightly Less Difficult* (IVP), let's 'talk to God about people, before we talk to people about God'.

Clue three: Fuel your prayers
through thankfulness

Paul mentions the importance of 'being thankful' (Colossians 4:2). Thankfulness in prayer is the fuel that keeps prayer going. As we look back and see what God has done, it helps us to praise him in the present. It also fuels faith for the future for what he is going to do. One of the common problems in our prayer lives is 'unbalanced praying', focusing on only one aspect of prayer. Each of us has a tendency to do that in a different way. Healthy praying is balanced praying. It includes praise for who God is, reflection on the Bible, a willingness to acknowledge our sins, expressing gratitude for what he has done, a desire to say 'yes' to God in whatever he wants to do in our lives, and the bringing of our requests to him.

In the middle of this pattern for prayer is the all-important thankfulness. Paul reminds us not to skip over this, for as we recognize God at work in the past, it will encourage us to expect him to be at work in the future.

What can we be thankful for today? How has God answered our prayer for others? There is nothing like answered prayer to encourage us to pray.

Clue four: Pray for one another

Paul invites the Christians at Colossae to pray for him. His request gives us another clue for our prayers.

'Pray for us, too' (Colossians 4:3). I find it incredible that mega-apostle Paul wants this young group of Christians to pray for him. Why do I find that so incredible? Because I have somehow swallowed a lie that the professionals, the Christian 'superstars', our heroes, have got it all together. They don't need our prayers, we need theirs. How far from the truth this is, and how grateful I am to Paul for showing us something which needs to be central in our church life. We all need each other's prayers; we are in this together, it's a partnership.

In another letter, Paul writes to a church in Philippi and says, 'I always pray with joy because of your partnership in the gospel from the first day until now' (Philippians 1:4). The word for partnership means to be 'yoked together'.

During the summer holidays, we were doing a number of fun things with our children. We visited a Shire Horse Museum. Our eldest son was fascinated by the sheer size of the horses, but what captured my attention was an information board explaining how a single Shire horse could pull a one-ton beer dray, whereas two horses yoked together were able to pull 27 tons. Now that is partnership. Together we can do so much more.

The same is true in the Christian life. Paul knew that we are all in this together, yoked in partnership. Pray for us, he urges. Where in our church life can we regularly pray with others about playing our part in evangelism? For some, that may be their home-group, or at the choir practice, or even at the PCC, elders', diaconate or Church Council meeting.

Engraved on my memory is a visit to a church in southern India. It was their PCC evening that night, and I asked the vicar, 'What's on the agenda for the meeting?' He looked at me, a bit surprised. 'The same as always,' he responded. Expecting the usual array of buildings, finance, and a lengthy discussion on whether to increase the cleaner's wages by 20 pence a week, I turned up ready for a dull evening. I was amazed to learn that 'the same as always' meant an hour's prayer for those people they knew who weren't Christians. If that wasn't incredible enough, they then left their meeting-room to go and talk to those people about the faith.

When we gather in our church groups why don't we give part of every meeting to praying together for those we know who aren't Christians? Yes, it will need to be introduced sensitively, but it would make a clear statement about one of the priorities of the Christian faith, and also encourage us to keep focused on serving those who aren't yet Christians.

Clue five: Pray for God to give opportunities

'That God may open a door for our message' (Colossians 4:3). So we put aside time to pray. It may be on our own, or with others in a group. But what do we pray? For God to open doors. I need to issue a Kingdom health warning at this point. Such prayer can seriously affect your life. Don't say you haven't been warned, for it is my experience that if we dare to ask God to give us opportunities, to open doors for the message, he will be only too happy to oblige.

We are going to explore what the opportunities might look like and how best to take them in Chapter 4, but I have no doubt that they will come. God longs to use us in the lives of others, and I know that I can leave it up to him to provide the right sort of opportunities for me.

The particular opportunity Paul asks for here is 'for our message' (Colossians 4:3). Why don't we pray for the same sort of opportunities? It is crucial that we serve others by our actions and care for people in practical ways. Yet I believe we are called to back up what we do with what we say—to speak about the good news. It *is* good news after all, in a world that is so short of good news. People need to hear about the faith as well as seeing it in action, and the most likely place that people will hear about the good news of Christianity is from the lips of those they know and trust. Go on: dare to pray for such opportunities.

The problem I have with opportunities is that I often miss them, even the obvious ones. So, although it is not in this passage, I would like to suggest two other things to include in our prayers at this stage: eyes to see the opportunities and courage to take them. I don't want to see the opportunities after they've passed; I want to see them in time to take them. I also know that even when I do see them in time, even when they are staring me in the face so that I can't possibly miss them, I still struggle to take them. In a split second I hear myself rattling off excuses as to why this is not the moment to say anything. I am always amazed at how inventive the excuses can be, and how persuasive. For this reason I now pray for courage as well. I know that there is a split second of decision when the conversation could go one of two ways and it depends on what I say next. Lord, please give me courage at that moment—the sort of courage that led Paul to speak up about his faith, even in difficult circumstances.

Clue six: Pray for wise words and a clear focus on Jesus

'...so that we may proclaim the mystery of Christ, for which I am in chains. Pray that I may proclaim it clearly, as I should' (Colossians 4:3–4). Here is one final thing to pray: for wisdom to know what to say and an ability to talk about Jesus. Every situation will be different, every person unique, every occasion loaded with its particular joys and tensions. We need the wisdom of God to know what to say, when, and to whom.

I am not suggesting that we all have to be able to articulate the most complex theological truths, but simply to speak about the mystery of Christ in ways that are clear and helpful to the person who is listening. We are going to explore how to do this in Chapters 5, 6 and 7.

Putting it into practice

Here are Paul's clues to help us pray, recognizing that prayer helps us to see things as God sees them.

- Clue one: Keep on praying
- Clue two: Focus your prayers through watchfulness
- Clue three: Fuel your prayers through thankfulness
- Clue four: Pray for one another
- Clue five: Ask God to give opportunities
- Clue six: Ask God for wisdom and an ability to focus on Jesus

Occasionally I meet people who have been praying for someone to become a Christian for twenty, thirty, even forty years. I ask them how they have kept going over that time, what has sustained them and inspired them to keep on praying. Their responses are surprisingly similar. 'Praying for one step at a time... being thankful for every answer to prayer... being able to pray with others... being able to let go and trust God for the opportunities...' They've learnt over the years something that a good friend of mine has more recently learnt, and what Paul is trying to encourage those early Christians all those years ago to learn.

It all started with a prayer

Miriam and I used to work together. We were both a part of a staff team for a church. When I was appointed I think she was quite pleased. Evangelism wasn't 'her thing' and now there was someone on the staff who was obviously excited about evangelism. It was definitely 'his thing'. We got on well, and over the years we worked together I learnt much from her.

I remember clearly a key moment in her own experience. She was on a Christian conference, one of those ones with dozens of different seminars. She wasn't particularly attracted by any of them, and strangely found herself going to one on evangelism. The man leading the seminar spoke about evangelism in a way that made sense of it for Miriam. She was particularly interested when he suggested that the best starting point was prayer. Now prayer was Miriam's thing. He suggested they thought of someone they knew who wasn't a Christian and prayed for them regularly. Miriam had a number of people in mind, one of whom lived down her street.

The speaker went on. 'So what are you going to pray for this person?' Miriam thought, 'Well, I suppose I ought to pray that they become a Christian.' The speaker said, 'Some of you are probably thinking that you should pray they become a Christian.' 'Yes,' thought Miriam. 'Can you believe that is going to happen?' said the speaker. 'No, not really,' thought Miriam. 'If you can't,' continued the speaker, 'why don't you pray for something a little more tangible?' 'Like what?' thought Miriam. 'Let me suggest a few things…' said the speaker. He suggested they thought about the situation and prayed for the next appropriate step in their relationship with that person. Miriam didn't really know the person that well, and thought about asking her round for coffee. As the seminar finished, she asked God to give her an opportunity to invite the woman round for coffee that week. You can probably guess what happened.

On Thursday that week, she was walking down to school with her children when the woman came out of her house and walked with them. Half an hour later they were having coffee together in her home. Miriam was so thankful that she began to pray for the next step in her relationship with Kate. This was ten years ago now. What started as a simple prayer has now become a lifelong habit. I know Miriam devotes herself to praying for three people, being watchful and thankful, asking for God to give opportunities to share the faith, eyes to see them, courage to take them, and wisdom to know what to say. It all started with *a* prayer.

Devote yourselves to prayer

Dorothy, like my friend Miriam, wasn't sure where to start. Paul would urge her to pray. It is certainly a reminder I need to hear as well. To pray for God to open doors of opportunity, to pray for eyes to see them, courage to take them, wisdom to know what to say. To allow my prayers to be fuelled by thankfulness and focused by watchfulness. To be attentive to God's inner prompting —those occasions when I sense it would be a good idea to phone John or talk to Sam. To pray with others so that they can encourage me and I them.

Above all, says Paul, 'keep on praying'. For as we pray we'll see things as God sees them, and our attitudes and actions will be

moulded by him. And as we talk to God about people, we will discover more and more opportunities to talk to people about God.

To consider

What motivates you to talk about your faith with others? What demotivates you? How can you increase the former and decrease the latter?

If you are unsure who to pray for, the following exercise may help. Ask God who you could pray for—someone who isn't yet a Christian—then follow the guidelines below.

- Under the headings Family, Colleagues, Neighbours, Friends, and Acquaintances (i.e. through hobbies, sports, interests), write down the names of all the people you are in regular contact with (at least one face-to-face encounter a fortnight).
- Identify those who are already Christian by underlining them.
- From the remainder, prayerfully choose one to three people who you can pray for.
- Don't be surprised if it takes time to settle on the right people.
- Pray for them regularly. For some, that will mean once a week during the intercessions at church; for others, it may mean every day.

A prayer

Heavenly Father, thank you for N.
Help me to see them as you see them
to love them as you love them
to care for them as you care for them.
Please give me opportunities to speak about you.
Give me eyes to see them,
courage to take them,
and wisdom to know what to say. Amen

Monday: Roger, at his desk

It was a single word. 'Privilege.'

Roger couldn't get it out of his mind. All morning he'd grappled with its significance. Naomi had said it was a 'privilege'.

'Penny for your thoughts?'

Roger looked up from where he had been blankly staring at the computer screen to see Mavis standing by his desk.

'Sorry, I was miles away,' he flustered. 'Been there long?'

'A minute or two short of eternity,' Mavis replied with a grin.

'What can I do for you?'

'I just popped by to see how things are. I haven't seen you for a while.'

'That's kind of you. We're just coping, but I'm sure we'll make it through.'

'If there is anything I can do, just let me know.'

'Thanks. What about yourself?'

'Great. We had a good weekend at a friend's wedding. This will interest you. The church was one of those places with a young vicar. He even had an earring. He certainly made us all sit up and think in the sermon, and had a group of us in fits of laughter after the service. If he was vicar of our local church I might just be tempted to go along.'

'Really... good... uuum... we've got a good person at our place. A woman, actually. If you'd ever like to come along, you'd be more than welcome.'

'I just might surprise you one day. Fancy a coffee?'

'Sorry, must press on. I've been staring at this blank

screen for too long, and if I don't get this report in by the end of the day I'll be in trouble.'

'See you around, then.'

'Yeah.'

As she walked away, Roger mused, 'Privilege; more like a struggle. Even when I do get an opportunity to say something, I never seem to get anywhere. Naomi would have gone for coffee and converted her by lunch-time. Why do I never feel comfortable talking about my faith?'

Chapter 3

One step at a time

On a scale of one to ten, where one equals hopeless and ten excellent, how would you rate Roger's handling of the conversation with Mavis? Given a similar situation, how would we rate ourselves?

My hunch is that Roger would have rated himself three to five. We might rate him five to seven. Roger feels as though he's hopeless. He never sees people dramatically converted; he rarely has a conversation about Christian things. The exchange with Mavis was typical. On the one or two occasions a year when Christianity does come up in conversation, it never goes very far, and normally ends with him feeling inadequate.

Roger doesn't feel comfortable. He thinks others would handle the opportunities he gets more adequately than he can. In his mind he remembers all the stories of those who effortlessly help others become Christians. He wonders what he can do.

In Colossians 4:5 Paul writes, 'Be wise in the way you act towards outsiders.' Here is good advice for Roger and for those of us who relate to his predicament.

Wisdom in engaging

Most of us have experienced poor treatment at the hands of a person, organization or institution. We're left feeling angry, dehumanized and frustrated, and are unlikely to return to that place for further contact. Sadly, many 'outsiders' have experienced similar treatment at the hands of Christians.

Jessica was in her sixties and fighting cancer. Walking from the hospital to the bus stop she found the weight of her bag and the

heat of the day too much. She staggered to a bench and slumped down, trying to recover her breath. A moment later two young men stopped in front of her. 'Can we talk to you?' they said, and before she had a chance to catch her breath and respond they launched into their Christian sales patter. She didn't hear much of what they said. A few minutes later, the two men walked off, somewhat disgruntled. Confused, angry, hurt and helpless, Jessica sat alone on the bench.

I met Jessica five years after this event and she told me the story of those two men, the anger and deep hurt still evident. They had left a scar, in some way, deeper and more damaging than the one from the surgeon's knife.

Sadly, I am all too well aware that people will have met me and also have been left hurt, angry and scarred by the experience. I look back with alarm at some of the things I have done and said. I may have had all the right arguments, but I certainly lacked wisdom and sensitivity towards outsiders.

In Acts 8:26–40 we meet Philip and an Ethiopian eunuch. The encounter between these two men provides us with a number of insights which may help us to be wise in the way we act towards outsiders. We don't know much about the two men. Philip was one of seven chosen in Acts 6 to serve at tables, to release the apostles to teach and pray. By the time we get to Acts 8:4–8 he is in Samaria, and having a great time. It's there that we gain our first insight into wise consideration of others.

In Acts 8:4–8, people are being healed, they hang on his every word and, because of what God is doing, there is great joy in the city. Things are going so well that the apostles send in the heavyweights, Peter and John, to help out.

Insight one: The importance of active listening

In the midst of all this exciting activity, God speaks: 'Go south to the road—the desert road—that goes down from Jerusalem to Gaza' (Acts 8:26). Now I can imagine my reaction. 'What, Lord?

Things are going so well here and you want me to go to a deserted piece of road? Do you know what you are up to? I'm needed here.' Yet, thankfully, Philip was different from me, and here is our first clue to active listening.

He listened to God's inner prompting & responded positively
I realize things were made pretty clear for Philip—it was an angel, after all. I don't rule out for a moment that God may use an angel to speak to us, but my experience is that he is more likely to give us an internal nudge: 'Phone Jane... Visit Bob... Talk to that woman... Pray for Andrew...' We may not be able to make sense of it, we may question why, we may rationalize it away as our own thought, but when we begin to respond positively to those internal nudges we begin to see God's doors of opportunities swing wide open.

God's prompting doesn't stop there. When he is travelling on his way Philip is prompted by the Spirit to 'go to that chariot and stay near it' (v. 29). Again I can imagine my response: 'Lord, have you any idea who that is...?

Let's try to feel our way into Philip's predicament. Picture the scene. You are at home, peacefully minding your own business. A phrase crosses your mind: 'Go to the park.' You ignore it, but it stays, somehow insistent. You can't think of a single good reason to go to the park. In fact, there are a thousand good ones not to. But something about this nudge makes you respond positively. You put on your coat and walk the two miles to your local park. As you wonder what to do next you see a group of people jogging round the perimeter path. There's a man slightly separated, ahead of a group of half a dozen very fit-looking men. They are foreign-looking. You're about to look away when a further nudge says, 'Go up to that group and stick with them.' Apart from the sheer logistical difficulty of keeping up, something makes you think that those men are not going to be too keen on you shadowing them. How do you respond?

If you are like me, you probably never even made it to the park. If you got to the park, running alongside this unknown group of men is a stage too far. You slink off back to your home, wondering what all that was about. God knows!

Strangely enough, he does. He knows that the man is the Chancellor of the Exchequer of an African country. He knows that the men behind him are his bodyguards. God knows he's visiting England because his childhood English tutor made a lasting impression on him. God knows it wasn't the tutor's teaching skills the man remembers, but the tutor's radiant Christian faith. God knows he's never been able to forget. God knows that the man has longed to track his old tutor down. That's why he's visiting your town, because he's discovered that the tutor lives nearby. God knows.

And God in his infinite wisdom has chosen you to be the one to talk to him. If you'd known all that, how would you have responded to those inner nudges? Sounds outrageous? It's not so far from what happened to Philip.

Being wise in the way we act towards outsiders starts with listening to God and allowing him to direct us—sometimes to the most unlikely places. It may be very unlikely that we'll be asked to go to the park, but what about the internal nudge concerning the new immigrant family at the end of the street, the person no one wants to be with at work, the man crying at the school gate?

Years ago, Martini advertised with that catchy phrase, 'Any time, any place, anywhere'. God is looking for Martini Christians— please, don't quote me out of context—any time, any place, anywhere. It's an attitude thing—an attitude Philip had.

God does know what he is doing. Trust him.

Philip listened to what the eunuch was reading

Philip runs up to the chariot and hears the man reading from Isaiah the prophet. Once again, it's rather given to him on a plate, yet he is wise, and rather than crashing in with some inappropriate statement—'You need to be born again'—he asks a question.

In our conversations with people, there will be occasional telltale comments which, if picked up in the right way, can lead to further conversation. Often the best way is to ask a question. People don't like listening to monologue sales patter, they'd rather engage in a good dialogue. Questions oil the cogs of discussion. Good questions open up a conversation, bad questions close one down. Good questions are normally open-ended and begin with words like 'What, who, when, where, how'.

Good questions are also free of arrogant assumptions and don't imply that we know better, that we are sitting in judgment over the situation. To hear the difference between these two questions, you'll need to speak them out aloud: 'Do you understand what you are reading?' (v. 30) 'Don't you understand what you are reading?' One word, but it makes all the difference. The first question indicates interest but the second question implies a put-down.

Asking good questions is a skill, but one which I believe we can learn together. It is also the bridge to the next principle in being wise in the way we act towards outsiders.

But before we get to that, I want to draw attention to another aspect of listening. You won't find it directly in the passage about Philip and the eunuch, but in my experience it is a crucial part of active listening. People don't only speak with words; their body language can tell us a lot about their thoughts and feelings.

This was brought home to me when I ruptured a muscle playing squash. I was in agony, unable to walk. Fortunately, one of our friends is a physiotherapist. A telephone call to her and fifteen minutes later I was lying face down, trousers off, on her kitchen table. Thankfully, it wasn't anything too severe and she decided to give me a massage to ease the swelling. Well, there I was, having my leg massaged with nice-smelling oils, when she noticed the two scars on my right knee and asked me about them. They are part of my story of how I came to faith, so a few minutes later we were

talking about Christianity and I was asking her some questions about her background and experience. It was bizarre. We were talking about something really important and I couldn't see her face. I had no clue as to how she was reacting to my gentle questioning. It was then that I realized how much I depend on body language when talking to people.

If in the course of a conversation someone is uncomfortable, hurt, cross, confused or defensive, it is likely to show itself in their body language. Reading the signs can help us to engage well with the person, to ask a clarifying question, to apologize, to press a point home, to inject some humour.

The importance of active listening is the first insight for wise engagement with outsiders.

Insight two: Start where they are

Starting where people are enables us to make connections. Philip 'began with that very passage of Scripture' (v. 35). One of the fascinating issues in our society today is the diverse ideas people have when it comes to matters of faith. It may all seem a bit confusing.

Words like 'modernism' and 'post-modernism' fly around. Anything slightly alternative is labelled New Age. We're told we live in a pick-and-mix society where people create their own faiths out of anything that interests them. Spirituality is meant to be big business, but the church doesn't seem very popular among the younger generation. There are no absolutes, everything is relatively true, so as long as it feels good and doesn't hurt anyone else, 'go for it'.

In the midst of all this change we've experienced over the last fifty years, some people still feel a strong allegiance to the Christian heritage, while others have no basic knowledge of what Christians believe or the Christian story. Core words at the heart of our faith—sin, God, life after death, Jesus—mean different things to different people, so how do we engage wisely with such a diverse range of outsiders?

Start where they are by discovering what they already believe. No one comes to a conversation about Christian things with a blank mind. People already have experiences, opinions, ideas, which form their perception of Christianity before we ever talk to them. Some will be positive, others negative. Asking appropriate questions will help us to identify some of those things, and as I'm talking with people the following three areas help me to focus my questions.

What is their background?
What is their spiritual background? Were they brought up in a church-going family? Did they go to Sunday school? What was their experience of religious education at school? Have they ever had any spiritual experiences? Have they been involved with other faith groups? What's the story so far? People's backgrounds influence their current perception of Christian things; by gently enquiring, we can understand a little more about where they are starting from.

What are their current beliefs?
What do they currently think of Christianity? Who do they think Jesus was? If they believe in a God, what do they think God is like? If they don't believe in God, what has led them to that conclusion? What do they think of the church? How would they define a Christian? What are their thoughts on the big three: who am I, why am I here, what happens when I die? Understanding people's existing beliefs helps us to match them against what we as Christians believe and to begin to explore the differences.

Occasionally people say to me, 'Oh, I don't believe in God.' 'That's interesting,' I reply. 'Tell me, what is the God you don't believe in like?' Nine times out of ten, when they have finished describing the God they don't believe in, I can say 'I'm not surprised you don't believe in God. I don't believe in a God like that either.' Then we can begin to explore where their image of God

came from and how it contrasts with God as he has revealed himself to us in Jesus.

What are the blockages holding them back from Christianity?
The journey to faith is commonly littered with road blocks which prevent people travelling any further along the route until they are cleared out of the way. Such blockages can be existing beliefs or previous experiences, but they also involve misconceptions about what's involved in becoming a Christian. For example, some people think you have to wait until all your questions are answered before you can become a Christian, rather than realizing that we'll never have all the answers. Others think faith is a 'leap in the dark' rather than a step in the light, and are simply not prepared to take a huge leap without having good reasons. Some think they are perfectly happy as they are and so don't need God, but this completely misses the point. It isn't so much about what we need but about what God wants for our lives. I find that asking people a question like 'What would hold you back from becoming a Christian?' can help to clarify personal blockages. Identifying background, beliefs and blockages helps me to see where to start.

I remember chatting to someone at a party whose first child was to be baptized that week. As we talked, I asked about his experience of church. He spoke of attending as a child but stopping as a teenager. We chatted some more and I asked what he thought a Christian was. His answer told me so much. 'A good person.'

I said, 'Do you think it is possible to be a good person and not be a Christian?' It didn't take him long to answer. 'Yes.'

'So what is a Christian, then?' I gently continued.

'I guess, someone who believes in God?' he replied.

'Do you think it is possible to believe in God and not be a Christian?'

He agreed. We continued down this route for quite a while, exploring possible definitions of a Christian, none of which held up. Eventually he asked me what I thought a Christian was. At that point I said, 'I imagine if we asked every person in this room for their definition we'd have almost as many different answers as people. That's why it's so important for me to go to the founder of the movement to see what he has to say. If anyone has the right to tell us what a Christian is, it must be Jesus.'

Starting where people are enables us to make connections with people. But it doesn't stop there. For the next insight in engaging with outsiders is crucial.

Insight three: Lead them to Jesus

Philip began with that very passage and 'told him the good news about Jesus' (Acts 8:35). In my conversations with people, I want to lead them to Jesus. He is the heart of the good news, indeed he *is* the good news. Christianity is not rules to obey, a philosophy to believe, or a religion to observe. Christianity is a person to encounter, so let's take people to that person. There is no one more attractive in the history of the universe.

That's why I was so keen to take the attention off myself and put it on Jesus when chatting at the party. By doing that, we avoid giving any impression that somehow we are above the people we are talking to. Instead we identify ourselves as alongside them, looking together at what Jesus has to say. Jesus said so many things which speak to the heart of today's world, and to the heart of people's lives. We are simply acting as an introduction agency: 'John, I'd like you to meet Jesus.' Although we won't, of course, use these words, introducing people to Jesus is always at the heart of healthy evangelism, and it's helpful to do that in the most attractive and appropriate way possible.

Insight four: Accompany them on the next step of their journey

The eunuch asked to be baptized. It may seem like a dramatic conversion story, but let's be clear, it isn't. The passage gives us the

background so far. Verse 27 tells us that the man had been to Jerusalem to worship, and verse 28 that he had bought a scroll of Isaiah the prophet. Such a scroll would have cost a great deal. This man was already interested in God—he didn't require an invitation to believe, just some information about the person in whom to place his faith. Philip made the necessary introductions for him and the man asked to be baptized—his next appropriate step on the journey to faith in Christ.

What is the next appropriate step for the person we are talking to? How can we serve them in helping them to take that step? For each person it will be slightly different, but once we have an idea of where someone is on the journey, we can think of ways to help them. Sometimes we will be able to do that ourselves, other times we may need to introduce them to someone else. Evangelism is not just about being there at the moment of conversion, it's about moving people along on the journey to faith.

When we look to accompany people, we need to remember this—one step at a time. I may help them take the next step, you may help them take the one after that. God is sovereign. He can work it out. What he asks of us is to exercise wisdom when we meet with those who aren't Christians and, if appropriate, to help them move on.

Philip—Jesus-like evangelism
Some evangelists don't have a very good image—pushy, insensitive, aggressive, forceful, arrogant, unwilling to listen. Philip, the only person in the whole Bible called an evangelist, shows us a different way—a way of engaging with others which, I'm sure, reflects Jesus' approach.

Roger's dilemma
At the start of this chapter, Roger felt that evangelism could never be a privilege. Two things fuelled this conclusion: he knew he

couldn't be like Naomi, and he thought he had to see people dramatically converted every time he spoke of Jesus.

Philip's encounter with the eunuch offers him a different perspective. He can start where people are, listen carefully, lead them to Jesus, and accompany them on their next appropriate step of the journey to faith. Maybe he didn't do such a bad job with Mavis, after all.

God doesn't expect Roger to act like someone else. He wants Roger, and us, to be ourselves. He wants us to do what we can do. Yes, we may be able to do it a bit better. Yes, God will help us, challenge us and stretch us. But if we are to be wise in the way we act towards outsiders, we'll need to be natural. Roger will never manage that if he continues to think he's got to be like someone else. He hasn't. Neither have we.

God doesn't expect Roger to see dramatic conversions as a direct result of every conversation he ever has about Jesus. He wants Roger, and us, to take things one stage further. Often we'll never know how we have helped others. Occasionally we may hear about how we've influenced others. Roger will never relax if he thinks it's all up to him. It isn't. It's up to God. He simply asks us to play our part.

A wise Franciscan friar summed it up like this: 'Be yourself, with God, for others.' Great advice.

To consider

What would it mean for you to 'be yourself' and play your part in evangelism?

A prayer
Heavenly Father, help me to
> *be myself*
> *with you*
> *for others. Amen*

Tuesday: Geoff, down the pub

He was never happier.

This was his place, his special place.

The smell, the noise, the anticipation of the race. His father had ignited his passion, and when he'd died Geoff was happy to follow on. The shed filled his back yard and the neighbours sometimes complained about the noise, but it was his refuge, a place to be on his own.

The pigeon club meeting was tonight. First Tuesday in the month, as usual. He found large groups difficult, but over the years he'd got to know three other members well, and they would talk for hours in the pub about breeding, feeding and racing. The landlord was always friendly, and the beer good.

'So what do you reckon for the championships?' said Nick.

David finished his pint and said, 'Oh, I don't know, but I guess Geoff here will probably beat us all again.'

Geoff smiled. 'There's lots of good competition. Anyway, Pete's been training hard so I reckon we're going to see some surprises.'

'What's that?' Pete had caught his name as he returned to the table with the next round.

'Geoff reckons you're in with a chance this year.'

'I might be. It all depends on the day.'

Geoff stood up. 'Back in a minute.'

On his way to the toilet, he thought about these three friends he'd come to know and like. Naomi's sermon was still fresh in his mind. They knew he was a Christian, that he went to church, but he'd never had a conversation with any of them about his faith. How would he ever get started?

Back at the table, as he sat down, Pete said, 'What else have we been up to since we last met?'

Chapter 4

Opportunity knocks

Here are my corniest Christian chat-up lines.

Driver to hitchhiker: 'So you're a carpenter. My best friend is a carpenter.'

Heart transplant patient to doctor: 'Of course, I've already had one major transplant.'

Customer to shoe shop salesperson: 'You need a good soul in life. How's yours?'

Pedestrian to lost driver: 'You're lost. So was I until I found Jesus.'

Blood donor to nurse: 'Giving blood is so important. I know someone who gave enough blood to meet the needs of every human being.'

Clergy person to financial adviser: 'Of course, the pay is not very good but the benefits are out of this world.'

Believe it or not, some people manage to use lines like these and get away with it, but most of us cringe internally and think, 'Never!' If lines like these leave us cold, how are we going to start conversations about the Christian faith? That's Geoff's question. He's shy by nature, but even with those he's got to know well, he can't see how he'd ever talk about his faith. Stirred by Naomi's sermon, there is a renewed desire, but he's concerned it will be short-lived, extinguished by the reality of never knowing how to start.

Pete, David and Nick show no interest at all. Geoff doesn't think they are necessarily antagonistic to Christianity, just uninterested. He can't see them raising it as a topic of conversation, so will there ever be an opportunity to talk?

In Colossians 4, Paul has already encouraged us to devote

ourselves to prayer, and to be wise in the way we act towards outsiders. In verse 5 he continues, 'Make the most of every opportunity.' What does he mean by this? Somehow squeezing Jesus into every pause in conversation? I don't think so. Manipulating conversations to include Jesus is not only unnatural, it's very annoying for those on the receiving end.

The word Paul uses for 'make the most' means to 'buy back' or 'redeem'. He is not speaking about creating opportunities to talk about Jesus, but redeeming the ones which already exist. Make the most of those, he urges, every one of them. Don't let them slip by.

What are these opportunities? How can we make the most of them?

Opportunities in the course of daily life

Let's accompany Geoff through his week.

Monday morning. At work Sonya asks, 'How was your weekend?'

Tuesday evening. Pete asks around the pub table, 'What else have we been up to since we last met?'

Wednesday early. Geoff is chatting with Bill. He meets him most mornings when he walks his dog. Bill says, 'I can't make sense of it. Whatever we do, there seems to be another famine in Africa just round the corner.'

Wednesday lunch-time. In the work canteen, Mary is reading the newspaper. 'Come on then, you two, let's see what's in store for you this week. What's your star sign?'

Wednesday afternoon. Bob's back is agony. 'I'm at the end of my tether. The doctors don't seem to be able to do anything about it, and at this rate I'm going to have to give up work.'

Thursday evening. Returning from work, Geoff chats to the teenager next door. 'I just don't know what I want to do when I leave school.'

Friday at his mum's. 'I picked up a little book in town today—
A Little Book of Calm. I could do with some of that right now.'

Saturday afternoon. After the match, Nick says, 'Did you see
that article about...? Said he's gone all religious.'

Sunday morning. Bernie's just moved in across the road and is
washing his car. 'Where are you off to so bright and early?'

'Make the most of every opportunity.' The opportunities are
there and Paul urges us to redeem them. They come in different
guises, some more obvious than others, some easier to respond to
than others. What will appear as an opportunity to one person
wouldn't be to another, but all of us will have opportunities. Here
are a few ways opportunities arise.

How we live

Our behaviour

For example:
- 'What is it about you? You are always so happy.'
- 'You've changed, you seem less anxious.'
- 'Oh come on, it's just a bit of fun. Stay!'
- 'Why won't you slag her off? She's a cow.'
- 'Why do you bother? Charity begins at home, you know.'

Our use of time

For example:
- 'What are you doing over the weekend/have you done over the
  weekend?'
- 'What are your hobbies?'
- 'Why are Wednesday nights never any good for you?'

Other people's lives

The cycle of life—birth, marriage and death

For example:
- 'We're having Sarah done next Sunday.'
- 'I don't want to get married in a church, but Michael is pretty insistent.'
- 'The vicar said he wouldn't marry a divorcée.'
- 'I won't be in tomorrow, it's Uncle Ted's funeral.'

Personal suffering

For example:
- 'They've given me my papers. I'm out of work from next Friday.'
- 'We're separating. It seems the best thing.'
- 'The tests will confirm it one way or another.'

Changes in life circumstance

For example:
- 'We've just moved in, new to the area.'
- 'What with the new baby, we are a little pushed. Our oldest isn't sleeping through yet, either.'
- 'It's probably the right thing, but I don't know how I'll cope. I'm such a private person and a nursing home seems such a public place.'

Life questions

For example:
- 'There's got to be more to life than this.'
- 'What on earth are we here for in the first place?'
- 'I'm sure if I had that amount of money I'd be happy.'
- 'It's ridiculous to think of it as anything else. Death is the end.'

Religious and spiritual items

For example:
- 'What's your star sign, then?'

- 'I'm reading this fascinating book called *The Bible Code*.'
- 'Oh, Mary's away this weekend, she's gone on a Buddhist retreat.'
- 'My faith is really important to me. As a Muslim...'
- 'Good morning. We're calling on behalf of the Jehovah's Witnesses. Have you ever wondered what is going to happen to the world if it keeps going the way it is?'

The media

TV

For example:
- 'Did you see the programme last night on genetic engineering?'
- Wasn't *EastEnders* good? What do you think Peggy should do?'

Radio

For example :
- 'That Chris Evans does go overboard sometimes, but he is a laugh.'
- 'Did you catch the *Moral Maze* yesterday?'

Newspapers

For example:
- 'Another depressing array of headlines.'
- 'What is the world coming to when...'

Magazines

For example:
- 'Here, try this questionnaire about finding your dream partner.'
- 'Did you read the interview with N? What a dark horse, so different from his public face.'

Moral/ethical issues

Personal

For example:
- 'I don't know what to do. I want to keep it, Sheila wants to get rid of it. Says she'll end up having to look after it and it's her body, her choice.'
- 'Dear, I want you to promise me, if ever I get to that state, you'll pull the plug.'

Business

For example:
- 'It's a straight choice between people and profit. It's clear to me—we go for the profit.'
- 'We've only got a small budget, surely cutting a few corners won't matter.'
- 'Tell her I'm not in.'

Society

For example:
- 'I'd expect more of government ministers.'
- 'But we, the council, don't have the ability to cater for the homeless. It's up to the voluntary sector.'

Some of these opportunities more naturally lead into saying something about our faith. I am not suggesting all of them will, I am saying all of them could. It all depends if we are prepared to make the most of every opportunity.

If we wait for someone to stop us on the street, look us in the eye, and say, 'Good sir/madam, what must I do to inherit eternal life?' we may never talk about our faith. Opportunities rarely, if ever, come like that, but people do talk about their lives, the

horoscope, ethical dilemmas. These are the realities of daily life. This is where we need to start.

How do we make the most of such opportunities?

It all depends. There is no pat answer. It depends on our relationship with the person, how well we know them and them us. It depends on the direction the conversation is taking. It depends on the context of the conversation. It depends on us being true to ourselves, trusting in God, and serving others. But saying 'it depends' doesn't mean we can't explore possibilities, as long as we don't think we are learning a patter, a formula. There's something very unauthentic about false sales patter.

One afternoon, I was sitting at home doing some work when there was a knock on the door. A middle-aged man stood there. 'Good afternoon, I was wondering if you'd given any thought to what's been happening in the world recently?' It didn't take me long to work out where he was coming from. I invited him in. We talked. It took half an hour, but eventually it happened. For an all too brief minute, I managed to penetrate the slick patter, to get behind the public performance with all the right answers and polished phrases. I asked him, 'What did you do before you were a JW, then?' and for that brief moment I could tell that this wasn't a question he'd been trained for. For a moment the shutters came down, and there was the real person. He stumbled, he mentioned the mess his life was in, and then, as if it was too much, up went the shutters and he neatly directed the conversation back to safe territory.

I didn't want a performance, I didn't want formulaic answers, I didn't want the party line. I wanted to engage with the person. As we think about what to say in the remainder of this chapter and the ones to come, please don't fall into the trap of thinking, 'If I just learn this I'll win through.' Anyone would rather engage with an enthusiastic, stumbling, unsure-of-the-answers but genuine person than with an automated machine.

The reason we are looking at how to handle opportunities is to give us a little more confidence, enough to get started. We can learn some things that will help, but we need to be real, we need to be vulnerable, we need to be honest. And if that means saying, 'I don't know'—fine.

Let's take two potential opportunities and, using the insights we identified in Chapter 3, work out how to respond.

Opportunity one: Sylvia
'What did you do over the weekend?' asks Sylvia.

The importance of active listening
Imagine Sylvia asks us this question on Monday morning. This is a potential opportunity.

Although, in some circumstances, answering a question with a question is appropriate—Jesus was brilliant at it—in this instance it doesn't appear to be the right response. Sylvia expects an answer to her question. Let's continue to be an active listener, listen out for God's internal nudges and watch for body language.

Where is the person starting from?
Let's say we don't know her too well. We don't know anything about her spiritual interest, but from what we do know we are fairly sure she isn't Christian. If we respond, 'I went to church. Would you like to come?' what is her likely reaction? A polite person may say, 'Um, no thank you' and internally be thinking, 'Religious nutter.' We haven't started where she is, in fact we've done just the opposite. We started where we are, with our experience of church and our desire for Sylvia to come and see what it is like. The problem is that when we say the word 'church', what we say and what she hears are likely to be two different things.

In our mind we picture the people we meet each Sunday for caring fellowship, vibrant worship, relevant teaching and great coffee (let's paint the best-case scenario!) In her mind, the word 'church' conjures up images of an ancient building, peeling paint, dank smell, freezing cold, old ladies, dull service and boring sermon, irrelevant to daily life. We can see why she may not be too keen to come.

We also asked her to come with us. How will she have received that? It depends, but here are two possibilities. Either, 'Me go to church? No thanks. Bit pushy—either they're desperate or they're after something, probably my money.' Or, 'A bit forward. I wonder if it's one of these wacky places, all singing and dancing. Not my scene.'

We can't win. Or can we? If we approach the answer by starting where Sylvia is coming from, we might just make something of it. First of all, let's get some balance into our weekend. Did we spend the whole weekend at church? Probably not. So what did we do on Friday night, Saturday, Sunday afternoon? If we mention some of these things as well, it shows we are a normal human being, doing normal human things like Sylvia does.

Secondly, when we mention church—and let's not leave it out—we could talk about it in a way which will raise questions in Sylvia's mind. For example, we can hazard a guess that she may think church is dull, boring and irrelevant, so we could say, 'On Sunday we did what we always do. We find it really enjoyable, and it sets us up for the rest of the week—we went to our church.' Immediately we've undermined all sorts of assumptions the person may have about church. We've implied it's fun and relevant, and also indicated that this is an important part of our life.

Lead them to Jesus

How Sylvia responds is up to her. At this stage the door has opened a crack. Whether she opens it any more is her decision. If it is

appropriate, we could give it a tiny push by asking a question at the end of our answer. 'Do you have much contact with church at all?' or 'What about you, do you ever go to church?' Now we are back to active listening and trying to discern where she is starting from. We're not yet talking about Jesus, but the conversation could easily go that way. Let's not force it, but let's not hold back when it is appropriate to lead someone to Jesus.

In general, I find it much easier to talk about God, church, religion or faith than to mention the name Jesus. I've asked other people about this and am glad to discover I'm not the only one. Why? Because when we name Jesus we are firmly 'nailing our colours to the mast'. That phrase originates from sea battles. When the captain of the ship was prepared to sacrifice everything to win the battle, he'd have the colours nailed to the mast, then they couldn't be lowered to indicate surrender.

When we name Jesus, we move out of the slightly more acceptable language of religion or spirituality. We identify ourselves as a Jesus person. People may think of us as fanatical, a Jesus freak, over the top. They may write us off as intolerant, bigoted and narrow-minded. That's why I'm happier to talk about God, religion and the church, but this principle reminds us that we want to introduce people to Jesus, just as someone once introduced us. For this reason I try to speak naturally of Jesus at the earliest appropriate moment. It nails my colours to the mast.

Accompany them on the journey

At this point we're not yet talking with Sylvia about deep spiritual issues. She may change the direction of the conversation, but at least we've planted a seed. That's one step in the right direction, one better than if we'd kept quiet about going to church.

If Sylvia responds, 'I used to go to church,' there are a number of options. 'What was it like?' 'Why did you stop going?' 'What impression of God did that leave you with?' Be aware that as the conversation continues our pulse rate may rise, our voice may change, and there is a tendency to become unrelaxed, and therefore unnatural, and possibly unhelpful. This is the time to pray silently, 'Lord, help me to be myself, with you, for this person', and to commit ourselves to serving Sylvia in her next step along the journey to faith.

Opportunity two: Graham

'I don't know what to do. I want to keep it, Sheila wants to get rid of it. Says she'll end up having to look after it and it's her body, her choice.'

Here's a second example of something that may come in the course of daily life—a very different situation to the first one.

Listen carefully

The words and the way this statement is spoken will convey a wide range of messages—confusion, conflict, hurt, anger, fear, embarrassment. This is not the moment to say, 'What do you mean? Of course she must keep it. Abortion is murder.'

I don't want to get into the rights or wrongs of abortion here. That is not the point. How we respond to Graham's statement in an appropriate way is our focus, yet we must realize that with highly emotive and controversial ethical issues like abortion, strongly held views have a way of communicating themselves, even if we don't say anything. Our body language, our tone of voice, whether or not we look him in the eye—all of these things play their part. Let's be careful. An appropriate response at this stage may be a question: 'Graham, would you like to talk about it?

Start where they are

What do we want to avoid? A judgmental attitude, naïve advice and simplistic solutions. What do we want to include? Genuine concern, a listening ear and sensitive questions.

The conversation is likely to operate on three levels: the conceptual issues of the rights and wrongs of abortion; the practical issues concerning what to do and how to do it; the emotional issues of the relationship and personal feelings. Start where Graham wants to start.

Lead them to Jesus

There is more than one way to lead people to Jesus. A minister I know, who does a bit of work with TV studios, talks about the many occasions when people at the studios tell him of particular problems they are facing. He offers to pray with them and has never yet been turned down. What better way to lead them to Jesus? In his thought-provoking book *Love Your Neighbour—For God's Sake* (Hodder, 1997), Justyn Rees explores this whole approach to evangelism, and offers lots of practical advice. He suggests it is best to pray *with* the person rather than just *for* the person. Admittedly daunting, he believes it shows the immediate relevance of our faith, and affects people because God is brought into daily life. Certainly that had been my friend's experience, along with many others who have spoken of taking a similar approach.

Accompany them on the next step of the journey

Compassion, practical help and prayer are a powerful combination. They open doors into people's lives, and Jesus walks on through. Who knows where this opportunity may lead over time?

The Jesus way

When it comes to making the most of every opportunity, no one is better at it than Jesus. He treated every person as unique. In his conversations with people he always managed to use the right analogy, image, parable, to lead them to himself. Jesus never processed people through a particular formula, he respected their individuality. Take a look at some of his encounters with individuals.

To the woman at the well he speaks of being life-giving water (John 4:1–42). To the confused religious leader he speaks of the

simplicity of childbirth (John 3:1–21). To an invalid man he asks a question (John 5:1–15). To the man born blind he speaks of himself as the light of the world—and heals him (John 9). With a distraught sister mourning the death of her brother, he weeps (John 11:1–45). With a woman wiping his feet with expensive perfume, he accepts her extravagant gesture and offers forgiveness (John 12:1–11).

There is no better model. If Jesus treated people like this, how dare we do any different? The more we develop a right attitude towards the way we engage with people, the more we'll find ourselves making the most of every opportunity.

Inviting people to an event

One other opportunity which may come our way involves inviting people to events run by the church. These will range from purely social occasions through to evangelistic events and courses like Alpha and Emmaus. How we issue the invitation can affect how people respond. If you do invite someone, make sure the event is going to be the right one for the person, and that you invite them in the right way. Here are a few ideas.

Be prayerful

Pray about it beforehand as you try to work out which event to invite them to. Ask God for both the right moment and the right words to invite them along.

Be precise

Make sure you know what's going to happen at the event, and then clearly inform the person what's going on, how long it will last, and who will be going. It's crucial that no one is brought along to an event with Christian input under false pretences. I regularly speak at events which have been put on for those who aren't Christians. Occasionally I'll sit next to someone early in the event and as I talk to them it becomes painfully obvious that they

haven't a clue there is going be any Christian input. I die inside. I know how I would feel if I had been invited to one thing and it turned out to be something very different. It just won't do to say 'Oh I'm sorry. Didn't I tell you?' Be up-front. Tell them what's going to happen.

Be positive
Suggest that the event will be good. Some people are wary of anything that smacks of church or religious fanaticism. Apologizing for the event is bound to undermine the person's desire to attend. Experience shows that there are three things most people are concerned about when invited to an event. They are worried they will be the odd one out. They are worried about being asked to do something publicly. They are concerned whether there are any strings attached. The more we can do to alleviate their concerns, the better.

Be practical
If they want to come, offer them a lift, or arrange to meet them outside the venue. Walking into a strange place on your own is no fun. If possible, leave them an invitation to remind them about basic details. Don't abandon them the moment you walk in. I've seen it happen so many times. The Christian leaves their guest alone: 'Just got to see someone, back in a minute.'

Be personal
Pushing an invitation through a door rarely works. Invite people face to face. It is harder, but much more beneficial.

What if they say 'no'?
Don't despair. At least we have asked in a way which enabled them to say 'no'. There are often good reasons. 'No' may mean 'not yet', or 'I can't because I've got something else on', or it might just be an instinctive reaction which they later regret. Beware of making it

into a big issue that they can't come. Ideally we should be able to invite them to a church event in the same way we would invite them to the cinema. This then leaves the door open for the future.

If they say 'maybe', in reality it probably means 'no'. Don't pressurize the person. Some people find it difficult to say 'no' when they want to. You could say, 'Think about it and I'll get back to you in a few days' time.'

If they say 'yes', let's do all we can to make it easy for them to attend, and keep on praying.

A final word
It helps to recognize that every individual is different. There is no tried and tested format for inviting someone along to an event. We must respect people as people. The invitation to an event organized by your church may be appropriate within a few minutes of meeting a person, or not for many months. Be open to God's leading and to a healthy dose of common sense as to what is appropriate—and when. And remember, it really is important to be ourselves. We need to use our words in our way.

Getting started

The harsh reality for Geoff is that he is unlikely to be asked a direct question about his faith by his friends at the pub. But he will have opportunities to speak in a relaxed, natural and helpful way about how his faith influences his life. So will we. The key is to be ready for them. A little forethought, a lot of prayer, and then we will be prepared to 'make the most of every opportunity'.

To consider

Take some of the potential opportunities listed in this chapter or, even better, ones from your own life. If you belong to a home-group, ask if you can work out a way to respond for each one. Alternatively, chat about them with a Christian friend.

A prayer

Father, open doors of opportunity and help me to see them.
Jesus, walk through these doors into people's lives.
Holy Spirit, guide me in what I say and the way I say it,
that others may come to know you,
One God, Father, Son and Holy Spirit. Amen

Wednesday: Alison, at lunch

Alison ferreted in her handbag.

'I'm sorry about the tears. You'd have thought after seven months I could control it a little better. It's like waves. One minute I'm fine, getting on with life, the next I'm sobbing uncontrollably.'

Margaret handed Alison a tissue.

'Thanks. Mine have all gone.' Alison managed a smile.

Margaret glanced at her watch. 'Please don't worry about the tears. I'm only sorry I've got to go. I've a meeting at two. It's been great to have lunch together; maybe we could do the same next week.'

'Yes. I'd like that. Thanks for listening.'

Margaret scooped her coat off the back of the chair. 'I'll give you a ring.'

Alison watched Margaret walk purposefully towards the restaurant door. She picked up her half-drunk cup of coffee. Just a few minutes more before she had to face work.

Seven months to the day. All the anticipation. All the expectancy. All the excitement. All the apprehension. All the pain. Then the most gorgeous baby. What joy they'd shared. Roger was ecstatic. Seven days. Seven exhausting, exhilarating days. Then nothing. No more crying. No more suckling. No more uncontrollable limbs buffeting the air. No more searching eyes. No more snuffling sleep. No more leaking nappies. No more endless washing. A virus, they said. Vicious. Nothing they could do. And Alison's world collapsed as she watched her seven-day-old baby die in her arms.

Samuel. They'd chosen the name so carefully: 'Heard by God'. They'd cried out for a baby. Five long years to conceive. Just when they thought it was hopeless, Samuel. And now where's God? All these years I've been so sure, and now...

Chapter 5

Have we got a story to tell?
(Part 1)

There's an 'Alison' in your church. Not literally, but someone like her, someone in intense personal pain, someone whose world has just fallen apart, someone who knows God but wonders where he is. Someone who has a story to tell, but is unsure about telling it. If you know the 'Alison' in your church, why not stop reading, put the book down, and pray for her, or for him. Right now.

Every Christian person has two stories to tell. One is the story of their journey of faith, the good times and the bad. The other is 'his story', the story of Jesus Christ. In this chapter we are going to focus on our story, in the next on the telling of his story.

This chapter may not be an easy one for you if your story, like Alison's, involves pain or suffering. Please don't feel bound to read it. I do believe that telling our stories is a powerful way of communicating the faith, but if this is too painful for you, please relax. There are plenty of other ways, and for the time being they may be more appropriate. If it helps, why not skip this chapter and move on to the next one?

Alison wonders where God is. It may take many more months, even years, before she resolves this issue. But the day may come when even she is able to tell her story, a story of God in the pain, God in the questions, God in the dark times. When and if that day comes, it will be a gripping story.

Why stories?

I am mad about motorbikes. I've ridden bikes since I was sixteen, and occasionally I treat myself to a 'drool' around a motorbike

showroom. My all-time dream bike is a Triumph. I picked up their publicity brochure on a recent visit: glossy purple cover, one word on the front—Triumph. Imagine my surprise when I opened the front cover and there was a double-page spread of a milk float. Not quite what I was expecting. All the horsepower of a lawnmower, the looks of a cardboard box, and the speed of a giant turtle. Standing next to the float was Fred the milkman. I began to read. Fred had been riding bikes for years; he'd always dreamed of owning a Triumph. In Fred's mind, no other bike would do. So he started saving (does this sound like someone I know?) bit by bit, month by month, until eventually... turn the page... Fred's dream came true. Picture of Fred with a gorgeous Triumph—just like the one I've always wanted.

Now you may be thinking I've lost it. But let me assure you, the advertisers know they haven't lost me. I'm hooked, because Fred is just like me, and by implication I could be just like him, standing outside my house with the bike of my dreams.

Stories communicate. They communicate well. They communicate in a way which is attractive, appropriate and accessible. Still don't believe me? It's confession time. Be honest, put a mental tick next to it if you like any of the following.

- Watching or listening to soaps
- Reading biographies or autobiographies
- *Hello!* magazine
- Watching chat shows, listening to talk radio
- Reading articles in magazines about people

Don't worry. You're not the only one. I've asked that question of literally hundreds of people, and the number of people who make no ticks are few. Why? Because we are nosy, or, if you prefer, we are interested in people. People's lives fascinate us. We share enough of their basic feelings, aspirations and concerns to be able to relate to them. It's why TV commercials tell stories, the most famous of

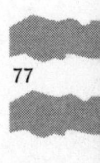

which actually became a book—*Love over Gold*, based on the Gold Blend adverts. It's why even the *Financial Times* introduces some of its most complex financial analysis with stories about ordinary people.

There's something more. Telling stories is also a way of communicating truth in an accessible yet intriguing way. We live in a society which is increasingly resistant to 'truth' claims. At its extreme, some argue that there is no such thing as absolute truth—often neglecting to see that their own statement is an absolute itself. People are suspicious of being told things in a dogmatic way—isn't that what leads to intolerance, fanaticism? There's a move away from explanation as the primary way of gaining knowledge to experience as the foundation of knowing. If you want to know something, you've got to experience it, feel it. In this context, stories are powerful communicators. Stories intrigue; they're based on experience, they're shared rather than preached.

Our stories are not the end of the story. There needs to be more than just our experience, otherwise we lay ourselves open to the charge of subjectivism—'That's your experience, but it's not mine'—but stories are a great place to start to communicate our faith.

What about our story?

Would you answer a couple more questions for me? Honestly. Question one: when you hear a Christian talking about their experience of coming to faith, are you interested and excited by what you hear? Question two: when you tell your own story of coming to faith, what do you think about it?

My hunch is that most of us said 'yes' to the first question. It is interesting and exciting to hear what God has done in someone else's life. In response to the second question, many of us thought, 'My story is rather ordinary, not very interesting, a bit dull.' Why is that?

One reason is that we've swallowed a lie—unless we have a dramatic conversion story to tell, we haven't really got a story worth telling. Even worse, because we don't have a dramatic story some of us wonder if we have a story at all. Take a friend of mine, for example. John and I were on a walk together and I asked him how he had become a Christian. 'Oh,' he said rather apologetically, 'nothing much to tell.' It transpired that he had been brought up in a Christian family, son of a minister. He'd always known God's love for him, and he hadn't even been through a teenage rebellion. That was it. He was embarrassed to tell his story because he was convinced it wasn't worth telling. It wasn't like the books he'd read, or the stories he'd heard at church. You know the sort.

I was lying in my cell. The heat was oppressive. Conditions were appalling. Solitary was hell, especially after two years. I know I shouldn't have hit the guard. I wasn't a nice man. Drugs, murder, theft, I'd done them all. A piece of paper fluttered in through the window and landed on the dirty mattress. I picked it up. It was a page from the Bible. I screwed it up in disgust and threw it in the corner. Six months later I spotted the paper again. I opened it up, and this time the words leapt off the page. It was John 3:16. I found myself weeping uncontrollably—tears of joy that God loved me, tears of shame for what I had done. Then suddenly the cell was filled with this light, and a voice said, 'Follow me.' The cell door swung open and I followed the light. I walked right out of the prison as though no one was there. I managed to get out of the country. Jesus rescued me from hell on earth, and hell itself. No problems now. I'm married, kids as well. I travel round prisons telling them about Jesus. Hundreds come to faith everywhere I go.

So I exaggerate… just a bit. But my friend was brought up on dramatic conversion stories, true stories. No wonder he thought his a little dull.

There are no second-class stories

Concerned that you have a second-class story? I've some good news. There are *no* second-class stories. However you came to a real faith in Jesus, it is God's unique gift to you. Born and brought up in a Christian home? Thank God. Slowly stumbled into faith? Thank God. Unsure of exactly when you became a Christian, but know you are? Thank God. Just a story of an ordinary life with Jesus at the centre? Thank God. There are no second-class stories.

There's more good news. I find the 'ordinary' stories often communicate best. Let me explain.

In my work I often speak at invitation services—services where people are invited along to hear something about the Christian faith. In preparation for the event I'll telephone the minister to talk about the service and ask if it is possible for me to interview someone about how they came to faith. The minister often responds, 'Now let me see. There's Jack—he was a drug addict, converted about ten years ago, incredible story.'

I reply, 'Sounds fascinating, but probably not Jack.'

'Oh, ummm, what about Sally, then? I think she was healed of cancer.'

'Amazing, but not Sally either.'

This may go on for a while, until the minister has exhausted his supply of 'dramatic stories'. Then, in exasperation, he'll say, 'Just what are you looking for?' I respond, 'I want to interview someone who has a very ordinary story of coming to faith.'

Eventually we agree on Linda.

Linda's story

I arrive on the Sunday morning and meet Linda. We chat a little before the service about the interview. She's never done anything like this before and she is shaking with nerves. I assure her she'll be great. Twenty minutes later she is standing next to me still shaking, dry-mouthed, wondering why she agreed to be interviewed. She tells her story.

I wasn't brought up in a Christian home, although we did go to church for the odd special occasion. If I am honest, I didn't really think about God much. After we had our first child, my mother insisted we should have him 'done'. We approached the vicar of the local church. He came round and chatted with us and seemed delighted that we were interested in baptism. He invited us to go on a short course to find out a little more about what was involved. It was just three weeks, and I actually enjoyed it. I think it was the first time I understood why Jesus was so important for Christians. The couple who led the course seemed to have something I didn't have. Anyway, Michael was baptized, but all our good intentions to go to church evaporated after a few weeks.

Three years later Susie came along, and once again my mum asked when she was to be baptized. I was so glad we had moved by then, it would have been too embarrassing to go back to the same vicar. We came here, and again we were invited on a course. This one was called Alpha. It was a bit longer. It's hard to explain, but during the course things really fell into place for me. I realized Jesus was actually looking for a response from me. I knew that I'd ignored God until then, but now I found myself wanting to take notice of what he had to say.

I suppose it came to a head the week before the baptism service when I reread the promises you have to make. I asked to see John, the vicar. He took me through each one and explained what they meant, that becoming a Christian is about entering a relationship with Jesus rather than being good or going to church. That night I found myself praying, asking Jesus to forgive me for ignoring him, asking him to help me follow him. I think it was from that moment on that things started to change. Nothing dramatic, but slowly, gradually, I realized my priorities and perspective on life were different.

I wish I could say that following Jesus has made life easy. It hasn't. Coping with Simon's redundancy has been tough. But I know that whatever we face there is someone with me, someone to turn to. Knowing Jesus really does make a difference.

Linda sits down, relieved. A little later I preach my socks off. At the end of the service I'm doing my vicarly bit, standing at the door shaking people's hands as they leave. 'Great service.'

'Yes,' I think to myself, 'I did preach rather well.' But the thing which they comment on that has made such an impression…?

'Wasn't Linda amazing? … That woman's story… What she said was so helpful… I could relate to her experience…'

I can't tell you how many times similar experiences have happened to me. Why? Because Linda's ordinary story could so easily be theirs. Stories relate well. Ordinary stories relate very well. I'm not for one moment suggesting that all we need is people's stories; as I mentioned earlier, it is really important to tell the story of Jesus so that we lead people to him. But let's not underestimate the importance of the transformed life story. We see it in John 4:39–42.

Another changed life

A Samaritan woman encounters Jesus at the well and is amazed by his willingness to talk with her, his answers to her questions, and his knowledge of her life. She leaves her water jar behind and rushes back to the town, seemingly no longer concerned about the very people she's been avoiding, and says, 'Come, see a man who told me everything I ever did. Could this be the Christ?' We are told that what struck them was her testimony: 'He told me everything I ever did' (v. 39). Is it too fanciful to imagine that they were impressed by her willingness to admit to things she had previously strenuously denied, despite the fact that everyone knew about them? Whatever, it was her testimony which brought them running to Jesus. They discussed with Jesus for two days, and then declared to the woman, 'We no longer believe just because of what you said; now we have heard for ourselves, and we know that this man really is the Saviour of the world' (v. 42).

This is a great example of a simple story of a life-changing encounter with Jesus leading other people to Jesus to have their own lives changed. Here is a model for us of how our stories can be used to do the same—lead people to Jesus.

A word to those with dramatic stories

If yours is a dramatic story, thank God. As it happens, mine is too, but we have to be careful how we tell our stories. The danger is, they can set up all sorts of unhelpful and false expectations. At worst, they leave people feeling, 'If that happened to me I'd become a Christian as well.' So when I tell my story I am particularly careful to focus on the Jesus at the centre of it, and to mention elements which could be part of their story. I often mention the many people I know who have come to faith in Jesus who have never had such an overtly dramatic experience, but for whom the reality of a transformed life is just as real. I want to be helpful for the person who is listening, not on some ego trip.

How do we tell our story?

There are no second-class stories, but there are second-class ways to tell the story. That's why a little forethought makes all the difference.

We want to speak about our faith in a way which will *make sense* to the person who isn't a Christian. That means jargon is out. Words and phrases like justification, redemption, washed in the blood of the Lamb and parousia are fairly obvious, but what about Alpha, Venture camp, home-group, gospel, grace, scriptures, the Lord? We're so used to them, we forget how strange they sound to others. Working out your story gives you an opportunity to eradicate any jargon or to make sure you explain simply any key words. If we don't work it out beforehand, I almost guarantee we'll slip straight back into jargon, because when we are nervous we retreat to what is familiar.

We want to speak about our faith in a way which *honours Jesus*. This is the story of how our lives were changed by Jesus, so let's not leave him out. We are looking to lead people to Jesus. Placing him at the centre of our story is a natural way of showing that he is at the centre of the Christian faith.

We want to speak about our faith in a way which is *lively and interesting*. Humour, illustration, connecting with people's experience, brevity, vulnerability, all bring life to a story. Repetition, exaggeration, irrelevant information, going on and on, jargon, all kill a story. Keep it short. I suggest two minutes for the basic story. It may sound impossible, but remember this is a conversation we are engaged in, not a monologue. Two minutes is quite a long time, and you can always expand in response to questions.

Here are two ways to construct our story.

Framework one: Before, during, after

This framework works well for those who know they weren't Christians and have become Christians. Under a heading 'before', make brief notes about your time before you became a Christian, a little about your spiritual background, beliefs and maybe the blockages for you as far as Christianity was concerned.

Under the heading 'during', note down the key points about how you became a Christian. What stirred interest? Who told you about Jesus? What did it mean for you? What turned interest into commitment?

Under a heading 'after', identify what difference being a Christian has made. Be honest about the struggles as well as the joys.

Once you've got a few basic thoughts down, try writing it out in full. This may seem unnecessary, but expressing it in this way helps us to see where things can be improved, and gives an opportunity to review and revise it. More importantly still, it means we can read it to a trusted friend for their comments. Don't try to learn it parrot-fashion—that's not the point. Once you've worked it out in this way, you'll find that a number of things will happen. Your confidence in your ability to tell your story will increase, because you know what you want to say and have worked out how to say it. Your ability to help others discover the Jesus at the centre of your story will also have increased. This is not just your story, it is Jesus' as well.

Framework two: Realize, react, result

If you can't remember a time when you weren't a Christian, like John, try this framework. The process is the same as the first framework. Under each heading note the basic points, then write it out in full and try it on a friend.

This time, under 'realize' write down occasions when you realized significant things about the faith. Maybe the first time you knew God's love was for you, not just everyone. Or the first time you began to understand what Jesus' death on the cross meant for you. Or your first recollection of answered prayer, or your first sense of belonging to God's family.

Under 'react', note how you reacted at that time. What were your thoughts and feelings? Why did you do what you did?

Then, under 'result', what was the result of that occasion? What difference did it make in your developing relationship with Jesus?

If it all sounds incredibly artificial now, it is! Yet without this preparation most of us will tell our story in a less helpful way.

If it sounds like a bit of work, it is. It's worth it, though. For, like Linda at that church service, your story may spark off genuine interest in Jesus for others. Who knows where that might lead?

When do we tell our story?

Occasionally we may have an opportunity at a public gathering like Linda did. More often, our stories are prepared to use in conversation with people. When a 'door of opportunity' opens, and a conversation has actually moved on to Christian things, we can ask, 'Can I tell you what happened to me that made me see

things differently?' If permission is given, we then take the opportunity to tell our story—briefly!

Again I need to emphasize, we are not to force our stories into conversations where they don't fit. No. If we are to be relaxed, natural and helpful, we need to introduce them at an appropriate moment and in an appropriate way. It may be a long, long time before that moment arrives, but if we have given some thought to *how*, we are more likely to see *when*, and to tell it well.

Why telling your story might be difficult

Please don't panic if at this stage you are thinking, 'I could never do this.' You're not alone. Some people find this whole concept of telling their story incredibly difficult, and you may be one of them.

Some people are unsure they have a story to tell

That might be true. You may not as yet have come to a point of firm faith in Jesus for yourself, or you may think you have but there's a nagging uncertainty. My suggestion is to try and find someone you trust, to talk this through—a minister or close Christian friend, or perhaps a complete stranger who is a Christian (sometimes that is easier). Allow them to help you come to a firm faith, because there is nothing more wonderful.

Some people struggle to talk about themselves at all

Low self-esteem, a painful story, crippling anxiety about what others may think, shyness, can all contribute to a reluctance to focus on ourselves. Please don't feel under any pressure to tell your story. If there are painful issues hindering you in living life, you may want to seek some professional help. Your minister may be able to advise you.

Some are going through such difficult times, they wonder where their faith has gone

Alison, at the start of this chapter, is in this position. She is from a Christian home, and she made a personal commitment to follow Jesus when she was fifteen, on a Christian activity camp for teenagers. She took a year out between school and university and worked as a mission partner in the slum dwellings of India. She led services at the church, occasionally preached, was active in her home-group and part of the leadership team. Then her world collapsed with the death of her seven-day-old baby. Just now, she's not sure where God is. She thinks that if she talks to Margaret about her faith struggles, she'll somehow be letting God down. Margaret isn't a Christian. Shouldn't Alison be joyful in the face of adversity, full of faith in the darkness? What is she to do?

She should be real—be real to herself, be real to God, and be real to her friends. Being a Christian is not all a bed of roses. Or maybe it is. Have you ever walked through a rose bed? It's full of sharp prickles with the occasional beautiful flower. Telling our stories without telling the *whole* story is only storing up trouble for those who decide to follow Jesus. Illness, tragedy, death, all continue to happen to the Christian. Jesus never promised to insulate us from the harsh and sometimes horrendous realities of this world, yet he does promise us a different perspective on these things—a hope for what is to come—and even more importantly he promises to be there with us, whatever we face. He knows, for on the cross he went through it all.

When we don't know where he is, God assures us he hasn't forgotten where we are. When we don't think we can hold on to him, God tightens his grip on us. When we cry out in pain, he surrounds us with his love.

The only story we have to tell may involve pain and hurt. Like Alison's, it may even be too painful to tell right now. Possibly we'll never be able to tell it on earth. But one day, when we meet up with the one who loves us and holds on to us in the darkness,

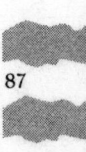

then, then we'll have a story to tell, and eternity to tell it.

Let's offer to God our story, and ask him to use it, like the story of the Samaritan woman, to lead people to Jesus.

To consider

Take time to work out your own story as outlined in this chapter:

- Choose a framework
- Write it out
- Try it out on a friend
- Revise it

A prayer

Father, thank you for all you've done in my life
Take my story,
use my story,
continue my story,
so that I may speak of you
and help others to have a Christian story to tell. Amen

Thursday: Tom, at the squash club

The squash ball hit the tin and Tom smiled. Not his night.

Shaking hands, Tom scooped up the ball and made his way off court.

He'd been playing Rick on Thursday evenings for two years now, and they could never tell who was going to win. Tonight was Rick's night.

'Tough game again,' said Rick as they entered the changing-rooms.

'Yup, I'm all done in. I'll have to give up,' Tom replied.

'I know the feeling, but I'm hoping to make it till I'm sixty. Look at Ted, he's still going strong.'

'I'll really miss it when I do stop.' Tom caught his breath and went on. 'So what did you make of last night?'

'If I'm honest, Tom, I was surprised. I enjoyed it. I don't know quite what I was expecting, not having been to anything like that before, but it was good. The food was excellent, and they were an interesting bunch of people. I didn't expect to see Nigel there.'

'We've seen all sorts of people over the last two years. That is one of the things I like about it—the format seems to appeal to so many people.'

'Tell me, why is it called Alpha?'

'Alpha is the name of the first letter of the Greek alphabet. I guess the church who started it thought it was a good name for something which is designed to start at the beginning.'

'And last night was a sort of introduction to the rest of the course?'

'That's right.'

'How long have you been involved at Christ Church?'

'Ever since I became a Christian. That's twenty-odd years now.'

'Well, that speaker, Naomi, certainly made me think. She put a whole new light on it. She was right, I have always thought of church as boring, irrelevant and untrue.'

'I know what you mean. I was the same until I discovered what it is really all about.'

'What do you mean?'

'Let me try and explain...'

Chapter 6

Have we got a story to tell?
(Part 2)

What would you say?

You're tired at the end of a long day and a tough game of squash. You've been praying for an opportunity like this for two years. Last night Rick came to an Alpha supper, the first church-related thing he has attended for decades. He seems genuinely interested. What do you say? What is it all really about? What is at the heart of the Christian faith?

Opportunities like this may not come too often. That's part of the reason why Tom is unsure what to say. Tom has longed for this moment, but is he ready for it?

I remember one such occasion. A small group of us were gathered for our weekly home-group meeting. Someone had brought along a friend who wasn't a Christian. He sat quietly listening for most of the evening. Towards the end, someone asked if there was anything he'd like to contribute. 'Can I ask a question?' We all nodded. 'I find it fascinating listening to you all, but can you tell me what is at the very core of your faith?' Seven very zealous Christians all opened their mouths at the same time and began to speak. One was emphasizing the importance of prayer, the next said it was all about the Bible, a third said worship was the most crucial thing, another chipped in with the Holy Spirit, someone added Jesus, and on we went. After what seemed like half an hour, but was actually three or four minutes, our visitor butted in. 'Another question please.' We all eagerly sat forward on our chairs. 'Where's the toilet?'

I have no idea whether he needed the toilet or whether he wanted to escape our seemingly incoherent babbling. What I do know is that we hadn't helped him much.

What do you say in a situation like that? Let's look at this in two parts—first of all to return to Colossians 4 and Paul's advice about our conversations at this point, then to make some suggestions about possible outlines we can follow.

A little salt, a lot of grace

Paul writes in Colossians 4:6, 'Let your conversation be always full of grace, seasoned with salt, so you may know how to answer everyone.'

Wise words. First of all, note that Paul talks about a conversation. Preaching is crucially important in the life and work of the church. I am not one of those who believe it is an outdated mode of communication. Done well, there is nothing to compare with it, but Paul is not talking about preaching here. Our encounters with people who want to find out more about Christianity are not opportunities for us to ascend an imaginary pulpit and let them have it with both barrels blazing. This is a conversation. That's why we looked at those principles from Acts 8 in Chapter 3 of this book; that's why we began with opportunities that arise out of normal daily conversations; that's why we disciplined ourselves to just two minutes to tell our story. Conversations, by definition, involve more than one person speaking.

Few people are called and gifted by God to be international evangelists who preach to thousands. Few are called to preach in church. But all Christians can play their part in conversations with others. Paul invites us to fill such conversations with grace and season them with salt. I wonder if we sometimes get this the wrong way round—'full of salt and seasoned with grace'.

I enjoy cooking. I may not be trained as a cook, but even I know that when the top falls off the salt cellar, allowing half the contents to empty themselves into the pot, I'd better start again. Salt flavours, preserves, and creates thirst. Too much and it is unpalatable, too little and it's unappetizing, just the right amount and it's delicious. Our conversation is to be seasoned with salt. We aim to bring out just the right flavour to leave the person wanting more.

It also needs to be full of grace. Grace values people, and treats them as individuals. Grace is willing to listen, even if what is being said is outrageous, ridiculous or untrue. Grace is prepared to go the extra mile, even if it is in the wrong direction, and to go at the pace the other person is walking. Grace is willing to challenge with the truth, even risking friendship. Grace sacrifices our personal preferences to serve others. Grace. Such a soft, gentle-sounding word, but one of the toughest things to live out.

Jesus on the road to Emmaus

Where do we turn to see an example of gracious and salty conversation? I can think of no one better than Jesus. In Luke 24 we have the account of Jesus meeting the two disciples on their way to Emmaus. This is the resurrected Christ. If ever there was a time for a bit of dramatics, this was it, yet look at the way he engages with them.

He gets alongside them

They are heading off in the wrong direction, away from Jerusalem where Jesus is appearing to his friends, and Jesus still walks with them (v. 15). He is prepared to walk at their speed in the wrong direction so that he can talk to them. Plenty of people we meet will not be walking towards Jesus. They won't even be interested. Grace means we slip alongside them, travel with them for a while, talk along the way.

He asks a question

'What are you discussing together as you walk along?' (v. 17). The resurrected Christ, the creator of the universe, asks them a question. Even more incredible, when they respond by saying, 'Are you only a visitor to Jerusalem and do not know the things that have happened there in these days?' (v. 18) he doesn't burst out laughing. The irony is palpable. Jesus may just happen to know one or two things about the events of the last few days. On occasions I've heard those who aren't Christians say what I consider to be ridiculous things, and the temptation is to laugh, exclaim, shake my head, point out how ignorant they are. It just shows how far I've got to go on the grace front. What does Jesus do? He asks another question: 'What things?' (v. 19)

He challenges them
Their reply reveals what they are thinking. At this point Jesus challenges them in strong words and speaks the truth about himself plainly (vv. 25–27). He helps them understand the Bible. Gracious and salty conversation does not mean we simply agree with everything everyone says. At the right time and in the right way, we will need to lead people to Jesus—we will need to tell his story. That's exactly what Jesus does here.

He eats with them
They persuade Jesus to stay a while, and in the breaking of bread their eyes are opened and at last they realize who he is. People come to faith in many varied ways, but at heart there is a life-transforming encounter with Jesus, which leads to a change of direction.

They are changed
'They got up and returned at once to Jerusalem' (v. 33). Lives turned around. Confusion clarified. Fear overcome. Despair dispersed. They proclaim the truth about Jesus. Why is it that new Christians are often natural and excited about sharing their faith? Because they have just encountered Jesus in that life-transforming way. Such a transformation is at the heart of the Christian life—an ongoing, life-transforming encounter with Jesus. It's why Tom, after

twenty years as a Christian is still talking about his faith in a gentle and quiet way, because he is still experiencing the daily renewing of that encounter.

'How can you motivate people to share their faith?' is a question I am often asked. Ultimately, 'I can't' is the only honest answer. The motivation has to come from within: the love of the Father, a transforming encounter with the Son, and the power of the Spirit. All I can try to do in this book is to take away some of the practical obstacles which have hindered us in the sharing of the faith so far. I hope that will help. What we all need, though, is the daily experience of God as the Trinity at work in our lives. I don't mean some spiritual high every day. I mean the renewing of our minds and lives which comes from a grateful submission to everything Jesus wants to do in and through us, a response to his grace that sparks a desire within us to share that grace with others, an openness to his Holy Spirit invading our lives. Seeing God's world and the people within it as God sees them. Allowing my character to be changed by that vision. Embracing a willingness to sacrifice my comfort for the sake of other people.

Gracious and salty conversation is not manufactured by us, it is modelled by Jesus. It is not something to be achieved, but someone to receive. It is not a formula to follow, but a person to follow. That's why Paul started this section of Colossians with 'Devote yourselves to prayer' (Colossians 4:2).

What do we say?

When it comes to telling our story, a little forethought goes a long way. It should be no surprise that the same is true for telling his story. Jesus focused on what the Bible had to say about himself. In the telling of his story we would be wise to do the same.

Let's return to Tom and Rick. Rick asks a direct question. Tom knows that preaching is out. He wants to speak in a way which is full of grace and seasoned with salt. He hasn't got the time, nor would it be appropriate for him to read the whole Bible to Rick, so how can he give an overview of what the Bible has to say in just a couple of minutes? Let's listen in.

Rick, if I had to try and boil the Christian faith down to its bare bones, I think this is what I would say. God really does exist. He's a loving God who wants the very best for our lives. He made the world and he is in charge of it. He made us to be in friendship with him and he's never stopped loving the world or stopped loving the people in the world. In order for us to have the best in our lives, God made Jesus, his son, ruler over the world and everything in it.

Tragically, we have all turned our backs on Jesus and that's why we don't have the very best for our lives. Some of us have done that actively, aggressively pushing Jesus out of our lives. The majority of us have done it passively, simply by treating Jesus as unimportant or as though he is not there. But whether we are really angry or couldn't care less, we have rejected Jesus as our friend and leader. The consequences are clear for all to see: broken relationships with God, with other people, with ourselves, and with the earth on which we live.

Thankfully, God has not left us in our mess. He does what you would expect him to do under the circumstances. God calls us back to him, to stop treating him badly so that our relationship may be restored. Jesus came into the world not only to show us what God is like but to make it possible for our broken relationship with God to be restored. That's what his death on a cross is all about. He offers us a new start.

Of course that means we have a choice. What if I won't accept Jesus' offer of reconciliation with God and a new start? It would be a great pity to be in this position, because I'd be missing out on so much. Eventually, when I die, I'll meet God. I will then discover that Jesus really was right. I'll miss out on living for eternity in friendship with God.

However, the best part of it is this. If I stop treating God badly and say, 'I should never have turned my back on you, I want to live my life as your friend and with you leading me,' God treats me as if I'd never pushed him out in the first place. God promises me forgiveness for all the things I've done wrong in life, a new start in life with him as my friend and leader, a sure future after death with him in heaven. I also receive a new strength to live as God would want me to (the Holy Spirit), and become a part of a family of people dedicated to honouring God (the church). He offers me meaning and purpose for living. These are all offered as a gift to receive, not as reward to earn. That's what I did twenty years ago, and although I can't say it has all been easy, I wouldn't go back on a single day.

Tom's response is a summary of some of the elements at the heart of the Christian faith. Of course much more could be said. Of course it is simplified. Of course it is emphasizing certain aspects of the Christian story. But he's made a start. His answer is based on a framework outlined in John Chapman's excellent book *Know and Tell the Gospel* (St Matthias Press). There are other outlines Tom could have chosen, some of which can also be found in *Know and Tell the Gospel*. They all have their strengths and weaknesses as ways of talking about what is central to the faith. I've found that the key is not to be restricted to just one.

A colleague of mine says that Jesus never preached the gospel. I know what he means. There is no one sermon Jesus uses again and again for every occasion; rather, he speaks the truth in a multi-faceted way, always turning the most appropriate facet of the jewel of the gospel to each person he encounters.

I recognize we can never be as versatile and flexible as Jesus. We can, however, do the best we can with what we have. Did you become a Christian last week? Then the way you'll talk about the gospel will probably draw attention to the facet of the gospel which most attracted you. That's fine. Have you been a Christian for twenty years, like Tom? Then your understanding of the jewel of the gospel will have developed. There are a number of aspects you

could choose from. What is needed is clarity and truth at the core of whatever we are saying. That's why outlines like the one Tom used can be helpful.

You may have learned outlines like the the bridge diagram, or 'Two Ways to Live', or 'do/done', or you may have been trained by Evangelism Explosion, or you may not have come across any of these. These are all outlines which can be useful and helpful. If you don't know any, why not learn one? If you know one, why not learn another? If two, try a third. If four... well, you get my drift.

I was talking about such outlines in a training session when someone called out, 'Surely these are too limiting. They are processing people through a particular formula for what they must believe.' He had a point, because there is that danger. But I believe that actually learning an outline or two should lead to greater flexibility and freedom. Back to Tom for a moment. Imagine he hasn't a clue how to answer Rick's question. What immediately happens inside Tom? He begins to feel anxious or nervous, his pulse rate increases, he's less relaxed than he was two minutes ago when talking about squash. Where is his focus of attention now? He's no longer concentrating on Rick, he's concentrating on himself, trying to work out what to say. His ability to listen well decreases, he's more likely to talk for too long, he'll hear himself using jargon, and when he eventually finishes Rick may be no closer to understanding what is at the heart of Christianity than the young man who came to our home-group that evening.

Because he knows an outline, Tom is confident about what to say. He can keep focused on Rick. He's listening. He can tailor what he has to say to Rick's own starting point. Outlines used well don't process people through neat formulae, they enable us to treat people as individuals. The reason why Jesus was able to be so specific in applying the multi-faceted jewel of the gospel to people's lives was precisely because he did know what to say.

Lost for words?

At another training course, one of the participants said, 'I always find myself tongue-tied when it comes to talking about my faith.'

We worked through various issues. We identified the importance of active listening, starting where people are, leading them to Jesus, accompanying them on their next step of the journey. We worked on her story, and on how to tell the Jesus story. We prayed. On the sixth week she told us about an incident the night before.

My husband and I were out for a meal with friends and a couple we hadn't met before. Somehow the conversation turned to Christianity and I can't even remember how. That old feeling came over me. I literally felt myself begin to freeze. Then I remembered to pray. 'Lord please help me to be myself. I trust you know what you're doing. Help me to serve this man.'

I decided to ask him a question, and as he talked I relaxed, and asked more questions. He was very intellectual about it all and seemed to have lots of hang-ups. He asked me what I actually believed. I was so glad we'd learnt an outline. For once I had something to say. I rather blurted it out, but he didn't seem to mind. He kept on asking questions and I did the best I could. At the end I suggested he might like to find out more from someone who might be able to explain it all more clearly. I am so glad we took the time to think about what to say. I wouldn't have known where to start otherwise. Did I do the right thing?'

Did she do the right thing? The other participants virtually gave her a round of applause! She did all she could and she did it as well as she could. What more could we ask? More importantly, what more does God expect? No more. He simply whispers in our ear, 'Be yourself, trust me, and love people enough to work out how you'll talk about your faith. I'll do the rest.' That's what Tom was trying to do.

Will we do that?

To consider

Try to work out what you would say if questioned about what you believe. Test it on a few Christian friends, or work at it together. Be sure to keep it short and jargon-free. If you'd like to learn some of the frameworks mentioned in the chapter, write to me at CPAS, Athena Drive, Warwick CV34 6NG and I'll send them to you.

A prayer

For your world, we give you thanks.
For your word, we give you thanks.
For your Son, we give you thanks.
For the cross, we give you thanks.

For our selfishness, we ask your forgiveness.
For our pride, we ask your forgiveness.
For our arrogance, we ask your forgiveness.
For the cross, we ask your forgiveness.

For your Spirit, we seek your blessing.
For your love, we seek your blessing.
For your direction, we seek your blessing.
For the cross, we seek your blessing.

Father, take us and use us for your world.

Friday: Simon, going fishing

There was a lot of uncertainty around. The factory workers knew no more than the newspaper articles. For three weeks everyone was on edge. As an apprentice, was his job secure?

Simon looked across the body shell. There was Bill, in his fifties. He'd worked here all his life and only needed another three years to get his early retirement package. Harry skilfully swung another door into place. He was in his forties and he hoped for promotion, not redundancy. Luke was the same age as Simon, an apprentice like him, just starting out. He was a serious bloke, always thinking about something.

The uncertainty was affecting them all. They had all survived the takeover, but now it seemed profits were not as good as predicted, and who knew what the future might hold.

Bill, leader of the small team, called time and they walked off to the canteen for a lunch break. Luke shuffled alongside Simon on the way.

'Are you free tonight?'

'Yup. Why's that?'

'Just thought I'd do an all-nighter. It is Friday night, after all. Wondered if you wanted to come.'

'Pick you up at eight?'

'Fine.'

As always, the car was laden with fishing tackle. Luke took it very seriously. Simon just managed to squeeze his rods in, climbed in the car and they shot off.

'Where are we going tonight?' asked Simon.

'Thought we'd try Travis. I've had some good nights fishing there. Bit tense at work today.'

'Not surprising under the circumstances. We should know on Monday.'

'What will you do if you're made redundant?'

Simon stared at the car headlights coming the other way. Strangely, he felt at ease about the situation. He'd been praying. Of course he didn't want to lose his job, but somehow he knew God was with him. He couldn't say that to Luke, could he? He'd just laugh in his face.

'Look for something else, I suppose. What about you?'

'I dunno. Never really liked the job anyway. Don't want to end up like me dad. I sometimes wonder why we bother. He's been at it for years and where's it got him? I saw this poster on my way over. It said, "Life going nowhere—nowhere to go?" and I thought to myself, "Too bloody right." Have any of us a clue what it's all about?'

Simon swallowed hard.

Chapter 7

Questions, questions, questions

Simon is unsure what to say.

There's some good news and there's some bad news for Simon. The good news is this: the number of questions he is ever likely to be asked about his faith is actually fairly limited. Given an hour's work on each, he will probably be able to satisfactorily answer ninety per cent of people who ever ask him those questions. Most people have not thought long and hard about the question they ask. That's the good news.

Now for the bad. Few people will ask Simon a direct question about his faith, and when they do it is likely to be a part of a conversation Simon has initiated about spiritual matters. That's why we have focused on how to make the most of opportunities. In everyday conversation people's questions are more life-focused than faith-focused. Here are a few questions in both categories, though of course the way they are phrased will be different for every person.

Common questions about life

- What is life all about?
- How do I cope with this sense of being so alone?
- Who am I?
- How can I deal with those things I regret in life?
- Where do we find true happiness?
- Why do I feel empty inside?

- Why do people suffer so much?
- Why is the world/my life in such a mess?
- What does happen after we die?
- Is there life out there?
- What's really true?
- What is love?

Most people ask 'life questions' at some point. When and how is different for each person, but ask them they will, often at times of crisis or tragedy. I remember one such occasion when I was minister of a church.

Fred died unexpectedly. He'd been invited to speak at the senior citizen s' club. He'd looked fine at the start of his talk, but after a few moments he asked for water, and then he sat down. Within minutes he was dead.

His family was stunned. I visited them the next day, Mum and three sons. We talked, we cried, we sat in silence. A week later I took the funeral and afterwards they kindly invited me back for refreshments. I was standing in the hall when the middle son came up to me and said, 'I'm a successful man. I have a great job, lots of money, foreign holidays every year, a lovely wife, two lovely children. I ask myself, what's it all for?' With that he walked off.

It's not only in moments of crisis or tragedy that people ask the bigger questions of life, but certainly in crisis many people find themselves questioning. Some may ask questions about faith, but the majority ask questions about life. These are more likely to be the presenting question that we have to address. Handled well, they may lead to the next set of questions.

Common questions about faith

- Why should I bother?
- How can you know God exists?

- What about other religions?
- What about the record of the church?
- Surely science has disproved Christianity?
- Why does God allow suffering?
- Aren't all good people Christians?
- Surely it doesn't matter what you believe as long as you're sincere?
- You can't trust the Bible, can you?
- Do you believe in hell?

These questions are never far from the surface when you talk with people about the faith. There are a thousand variations on each one, but only a dozen or so questions that the majority of people are ever likely to ask. Answering them well clears the blockages on the path to faith; avoiding them leaves people with what are perceived as insurmountable obstacles or, even worse, excuses not to bother.

How can we tackle such questions?

Let's return to Colossians 4. Paul ends verse 6 with these words: '...so that you may know how to answer everyone.' Do you think it's possible to be so well prepared and thought-through that we have an answer for every question we are ever going to be asked about the faith? No, I don't either. Nor does Paul. The whole of this passage has focused on motivation and mindset rather than methodology. Paul hasn't set out his ten top tips for answering people's questions (methodology), he has focused on his understanding of what will keep us going in sharing the faith (motivation) and the attitude we ought to have towards those who aren't yet Christians (mindset). He knows that if we get these two things right, we will deal well with whatever gets thrown at us and whomever we meet.

'So you may know how to answer everyone' is a statement of

result. Live like this, and this will happen. You may not have all the clever intellectual answers, philosophical arguments or rhetorician's skills, but you will love people enough to serve them and ensure their questions are dealt with sensitively, thoughtfully, genuinely. *How we engage* is as important as *what we say*.

What about the question we can't answer?

The day will come when we don't have an answer to a direct question. That may be your biggest fear and, like Simon, you dodge questions to avoid the embarrassment of not knowing. Simon thinks he'll let God down, but not having the answer isn't the main problem—the important point is how we handle not having an answer.

Here are some options. First and foremost, we must be prepared to tell the truth. If we don't know the answer to a person's question, we must be honest. We can either try to find the answer and use it as an opportunity to talk to the person again at a later stage, or we can introduce them to someone else who knows a bit more than us, or who simply has the gifts to deal with a thoughtful questioner. We could suggest a book they might like to read on the subject. The least helpful option is to say you haven't a clue and then do nothing about it. Love goes the extra mile. If the person is genuinely concerned about this matter, then we need to be concerned as well. In this way we will ultimately answer anyone who asks.

I remember an interview with Cliff Richard from years ago. At the time, he was speaking a lot in schools about his Christian faith. The interviewer asked, 'What do you do when you can't answer a question?' He replied, 'Tell them the truth: I don't know. Then I assure them I'll find out and try to let them know. I make sure I'm not caught out on that question ever again by going away and finding out what to say.' I was impressed. That's exactly the attitude Paul is looking for in his readers. The bottom line is not how much do you know, but how much do you care?

How to answer well

Between two jobs I had the opportunity to work-shadow John Chapman, an Australian evangelist, for a month. I learnt a huge amount through that experience. John combines an exceptional mind with a passionate heart and a caring spirit. He not only taught me the following principles about how to handle people's questions, he lived them out.

Does the answer lead towards the good news about Jesus?

Answering these common questions removes the road blocks on the journey to faith. Answers which focus on Jesus are helpful because they make it clear where the road leads. For example, if asked, 'How can you know God exists?' there is a range of possible answers.

- Creation: we could argue that our own existence and the incredible balance in the universe points to a designer behind it all.
- Experience: we could talk about the way we have experienced God and the difference he makes in our life.
- Bible: we could focus on what the Bible has to say about God.
- Jesus: we could start with Jesus as the one who reveals God to us.

All these are good options, but one leads more quickly to Jesus than the rest. How can we know God exists? Surely it would only be possible if God chose to reveal himself to us in a way we could understand. That's exactly the claim at the heart of the Christian faith. Jesus is God in human form, God making himself known in a way we can understand.

Note that each of these four options will lead the conversation down a particular path. If we choose the creation option, we're likely to end up talking about creation versus evolution, or science and Christianity. If we take our personal experience as the way in, we are likely to face the subjectivism issue: 'That's fine for you but

I haven't experienced that.' If we take the Bible as our chosen preference, we're likely to end up discussing the trustworthiness of the Bible. Finally, if we take Jesus as our approach, the key issue is likely to be the identity of Jesus himself. Was he God or just another great religious leader, one among many? So whichever path we choose, we need to be prepared for the likely issue behind it. All these approaches are valid, and all these issues may need tackling, yet I've found that nine times out of ten I go for the Jesus option. It takes me straight to the heart of the good news about Jesus and that's the place I prefer to be.

Does the answer sound believable?

In our desire to affirm how good faith is, we must avoid presenting a picture of a life without problems. It needs to sound believable to the person struggling with the everyday reality of life. We need to be real about our struggles, questions and doubts as Christians, while not denying the wonderful reality of a relationship with God.

Does the answer meet the real issue behind the question?

The question may be straightforward or behind it there may be something far more complex. In a pub I was recently asked what Christians thought of suicide. I didn't know the person—I'd only just been introduced as a minister by a Christian friend. I was about to plunge into a logical answer for the Christian position on suicide, when thankfully something prompted me to hang back. I muttered a few generalities and then asked the person why they asked. 'My father committed suicide six months ago and I wondered where he was now.' Thank goodness I hadn't ploughed on, but rather found out what was behind the presenting question. The issue was far bigger than I'd expected. This is one of the occasions when I got it right but there have been many others where I've got it wrong. One is indelibly imprinted on my consciousness. I tell it to make a crucial point.

A small group of us met for three weeks to talk about the Christian faith. I was the only Christian and the others were wanting to find out about Christianity. Dave was a man in his twenties who had a reputation for vandalism and violence. Now married, with a child, he'd calmed down and was attending the group with his wife. At the end of the third evening, we were drinking coffee when he said in his fairly light-hearted manner, 'What about suffering? Why does God allow that to happen?' I launched off into my carefully reasoned explanation of the problem of suffering. Out of my 'mental computer' came the answer (although I did realize there was no completely satisfactory way of answering this question). He listened to me rattle on. Eventually, when I stopped, thinking that I'd done quite a good job, he looked up and said, 'My sister died of cancer last year, twenty-one years old. It's destroyed my mother, devastated our family, and I can't see a loving God allowing that to happen.' You can imagine how I felt. I'd given a philosophical answer. He'd asked a personal question. The reason why I stopped myself at the bar was the lesson I learnt from this earlier experience.

Every alarm bell in heaven should ring in our minds when we are asked a question about suffering. Often, very often, behind the question is a pain-filled personal reality. What's needed is a place for the person to express their hurt, anger, pain and confusion, not some slick philosophical answer. Yes, we do need to work through how to answer this difficult question. Yes, we will have to learn ways of handling it well, but please be aware of what may be behind the question. I normally answer a question about suffering by asking whether there is a particular reason why the person asked it. If they answer 'no', I am still very careful about my answer, because sometimes the pain is so profound they can't even admit it. Let's be careful. We're dealing with people's lives.

Does the answer sound caring?
Some issues are very painful, delicate or sensitive. How can we talk

about the reality of hell without a lump in our throat? How can we talk about the pain of suffering without a tear in our eye? How can we talk about ethical dilemmas without questions in our mind? These things should not pass our lips without first engaging our minds and affecting our hearts.

Does the answer sound respectful?
We may disagree with the person we're speaking to. That is not a problem if we have treated them with respect throughout the conversation. Let's not forget, we can win an argument and lose a friend.

Does the answer sound arrogant?
It is so easy to come across as arrogant or condescending. Be genuinely interested in the person. It may be the hundredth time we have heard that question asked, but it may be the first time that person has ever asked it. Take time to answer. We need to think about it because we ought to be engaging with their particular question, not just the question in general. Beware of implying that we've got all the answers and that they just need to learn from us. Jesus was always humble.

What about the smokescreen or the red herring?
I'm often asked this, but in my experience I don't find that too many people ask questions for the sake of asking questions. People normally have better things to do with their time. If we are unsure, we can ask them a question like this: 'If I answered all your questions satisfactorily, are you serious about finding out more about Christianity?' Sometimes people are honest enough to answer 'no'. Don't write them off at this moment. Indeed, the way we handle this moment could be crucial in the ongoing process. Ask, 'Why do you keep asking so many questions?' Some do so to cover the real issue that they do not want to confront. Some do so out of a general interest in anything they don't know much about.

Some do so because they think it will please the person to whom they are speaking. Continue to respect the person, continue to leave the door open. If we think they are just making fun of us, politely but firmly suggest that we could both probably make better use of our time, but that if they ever want to talk seriously about the single most important issue in life, you would always be happy to do so.

How do we prepare ourselves to answer questions?

I've found the best way to prepare is to chat them through with other Christians. If you are in a home-group, maybe you could take one question a fortnight, or at choir practice take fifteen minutes before you start to sing. Try to work out how to address each question under four headings.

Explore what is behind the question

What do people who aren't Christian already believe, think or feel about the question? People don't come to these questions with completely empty minds. They already have views, impressions, prejudices and feelings. What are they likely to be? Identifying these things enables us to address each question more accurately.

For example, consider the question, 'Aren't all good people Christians?' Many people believe that a Christian is in essence someone who is good—who, perhaps, obeys the Ten Commandments. They think you don't have to go to church to be a Christian, and feel hurt or angry if we imply they are not a Christian. These are the assumptions people have before they even start talking about the issue. Each of these assumptions is misguided, inaccurate and unhelpful, but they don't know that. We can help them by exploring the issues in a way which identifies their misconceptions and offers an alternative perspective.

111

Express what Christians believe

Once we've begun to explore the question and the person's misconceptions, it may be the moment to express what Christians believe—the central truths at the heart of a Christian perspective on the question.

With the question 'Aren't all good people Christians?' there are four key things to focus on.

- What is a Christian?
- How do we define 'good'?
- What is sin?
- Is being sincere enough?

Each of these takes us to the heart of a central Christian truth. Many people misunderstand what a Christian is. The common misconceptions are that a Christian is someone who is good, believes in God, goes to church, or prays. Christians, however, know that it is possible to believe in God and not be a Christian, to be good and not be a Christian, to pray or go to church and not be a Christian. We may explore what goodness and sin are. Again, there are so many popular misconceptions. For example, people often regard sin as 'something other people do'—the really bad things. We need to clarify such issues in a way which helps people begin to understand God's perspective.

Identify supporting evidence

When we've talked a little about what we believe, people often want some evidence which backs up our explanation. They want to know why we believe that. Again, with the question 'Aren't all good people Christians?' we can point out how many good people we know who themselves wouldn't claim to be Christians, or we can identify people we know who believe in God, but are Muslims. Providing people with reasons for why we believe what we believe is important. So many people think that faith involves committing intellectual suicide, believing when we have no good reasons for doing so. Although we know there is mystery at the heart of our faith (see Colossians 4:3), that doesn't mean we can't use our minds to grapple with some of the complex questions people are rightfully asking.

Back it up with personal experience

The fourth thing which helps people with their questions is our own experience. In what ways has our relationship with Jesus changed our thinking on this question? Perhaps we can talk about how we used to think that being a Christian was about being good, but now we recognize it's about a relationship with God, one that is dependent on admitting we've got things wrong. Alternatively, you may be able to mention someone else's experience to illustrate how people change.

Questions, questions, questions

Using these four tools can help us address any question we may be asked. It does take time to think through each question and work out an appropriate response. But if we are really concerned to help others, then surely we will commit ourselves to some creative thinking to be prepared for the day when the question may be asked. Remember, most people tend to ask fairly predictable questions. A little preparation and we can be ready to answer.

We are not in this alone. Why not ask if you can discuss these sorts of issues whenever you meet regularly with other Christians? The impetus may need to come from you, but I am sure others will be grateful for the suggestion once they begin to see the benefits.

Simon feared questions, but the reality is that people will have questions. Initially they are more likely to be questions about life than about faith. That was Simon's situation. It may be ours too.

To consider

Create your own list of common questions about life and faith, ones which you've experienced. Take one at a time and:

- explore what is behind the question
- express what Christians believe
- identify supporting evidence
- back it up with personal experience

You could do this on your own or with others.

If you'd like a leaflet on possible answers to the common questions about Christianity, please contact CPAS.

A prayer
Jesus, on the cross you asked, 'Why...?'
Fill us with compassion
    that we might feel the 'Why...?'
Fill us with humility
    that we might hear the 'Why...?'
Fill us with grace and truth
    that we might explore the 'Why...?'
So that we might know how to answer everyone. Amen

Saturday: Injit, at work

The door closed behind him and his four-year-old thumped against it. As he drove off, the cries of his child rang in his ears and the look of disappointment on his wife's face played on his mind.

Injit hated working on Saturdays.

The Thursday deadline had arrived and he'd made it, but at a cost—the mounting papers in the pending tray. And now a crying child and a frustrated wife. Saturday really was the only way he was going to clear up the backlog and be able to start the week well.

Driving into the car park, he was surprised at the number of cars there—he wasn't the only one under pressure. He hardly noticed security at the entrance. In the lift, he looked at himself in the mirror. Tired.

As the doors slid open, that familiar feeling washed over him: this is my other world where I spend fifty, sixty, sometimes seventy hours a week. What was it Naomi said last week? Friendship evangelism? I'm not sure these people are my friends, but they are certainly the people I spend most of my time with. I wonder what they make of me? It's such a struggle to be a Christian here. It's all right for Naomi; she doesn't have to work with such pressures and people. Everyone looking out for themselves, profit constantly being pushed as the bottom line, expectations about the extra hours, bosses losing their rag, colleagues breaking their commitments. Just occasionally an oppor-tunity to talk about bigger issues.

There's Bob. I'd love to invite him to Alpha at our church,

but he lives forty miles away and I can't see him making the journey.

Injit sat in his chair, turned on his computer, and placed the pending tray at the centre of his desk. It was going to be another long day at the office.

Chapter 8

God at work

Work. The fitter on the factory floor. The council worker sweeping the streets. The volunteer at the charity shop. The executive in business-class, sipping his wine. The teacher grabbing a coffee in the school common room. The salesperson making yet another cold call. The sweating labourer on the building site. The frantic shop assistant. Work—paid, voluntary, recognized, unrecognized, valued, ignored. For those fortunate enough to have employment, a lot of time is spent at work or working.

While church leaders try to dream up creative ways of making contact with people who aren't Christians, church members spend the majority of their day rubbing shoulders with such people, Monday to Friday, nine to five, and the thousand variations on the working week. This is Injit's world, and it's not one he always feels comfortable in. One of the issues he faces day by day is 'What does it mean to witness in the workplace?'

He's not alone. People are concerned about this subject. Here are three examples.

- Barry sits in his car outside the factory. 'When I walk through those doors I feel as if God says goodbye. I become a different person.'
- Louise in the offices of a multi-national, at the end of an exhausting day. 'Why won't the church help me with the daily decisions I face which affect the lives of thousands?'
- Bob, confused over a pint after work. 'I try telling them about Jesus but they just don't seem to be interested.'

Much of the confusion about witness in the workplace stems from unhelpful theology which is perpetuated by our churches.

The church's agenda on work

To caricature the situation: Christians are committed to working for things of eternal value and significance—what is more important than the eternal salvation of a human being? Therefore, *real* Christian work equals being a minister, missionary or monk—'professional' Christians.

Where do we find this attitude?

In the language we use

'What do you do?' I ask.

'I'm in full-time Christian work,' or 'I'm in the ministry.'

Excuse me? Aren't *all* Christians in full-time Christian work? Isn't it the vocation of every Christian to work out their ministry in the context of daily life?

A colleague told me of a man at church who said to him, 'I wish I could get into a Christian job, as you've done, Mick.' His present occupation? He's a teacher. Isn't it shameful that he should believe his work isn't Christian? We need to move away from unhelpful language which perpetuates this idea that there are somehow 'higher' or 'holier' callings.

In the focus of church life

Most churches are essentially inward-looking. We draw people into 'ministry' positions, by which we mean positions which keep the church running, rather than sending them out to exercise ministry in the course of their daily lives.

In our teaching

A survey conducted by Mark Greene at London Bible College discovered that fifty per cent of evangelicals had never heard a sermon on work, seventy-five per cent had no 'theology of work' and only twenty-five per cent had been encouraged to see their work as a ministry.

In our corporate worship

When we pray publicly for people who work, we tend to select the caring professions—like doctors and nurses. Why don't we pray for solicitors, factory workers, child-minders, town planners, carpenters and farmers?

In our use of work skills

I sit in many church committee meetings. Often they are chaired by the minister, sometimes very well, other times not so well. On the latter occasions it is not unusual to discover, sitting within the meeting, someone whose company has invested thousands of pounds in helping them to set good agendas, chair meetings well, develop vision, and implement strategies. Why don't we use such a person to exercise their skills in our meetings? Or have we accepted the church culture—please leave your work gifts at the door, you're entering a different world?

God's agenda on work

These are some of the factors which perpetuate an unhelpful understanding of work. Thankfully, God's agenda on work is very different. He doesn't see it as a necessary evil to enable us to fund the work of the church. He doesn't see it as a foray into the wicked world of money, production and profit. He doesn't see it as secondary to the real work of the church.

God and work

In the first book of the Bible, we see God's creative purpose for the world. In Genesis, God outlines humanity's role: 'Let us make man in our image, in our likeness, and let them rule over the fish of the sea and the birds of the air, over the livestock, over all the earth, and over all the creatures that move along the ground' (1:26). God goes on to bless them and says, 'Be fruitful and increase in number; fill the earth and subdue it.' (1:28). It suggests that our work reflects God's work, and reminds us that work existed before the fall. It was always meant to be a part of life. As Richard Higginson points out in his book *Called to Account* (Eagle), work from God's perspective is 'proper management of resources for the glory of God, the benefit of humanity and the sustenance of the created order'. The call to be fruitful in Genesis 1:28 is not a call to evangelism, it is a call to be a part of God's creative purpose for his world. We will be held accountable for the way we respond to that call, for God has called us to be stewards of his world.

This grand image of the world does not match the reality we face day by day. The world is not as it should be. We declared independence from God and have made a mess of his world—our attitude to work can reflect something of that confusion. Yet God has not given up and in Romans 8 we see his redemptive purpose at work. The physical universe is destined not for destruction, but renewal. The work of God is not just for personal redemption, but for the universe to be redeemed (Romans 8:18–21). This redemption means a restoring to the original pattern, and should affect both how we work and the value of our work.

The big picture

Imagine you are in the heavenly planning-room. God the Father is poring over the eternal plans for the history of our small planet. The computer screen is awash with data and details. You sit down next to him and cough discreetly. He turns and smiles. With a deft movement of the mouse, the screen begins to change, the plans glide before your eyes, immense in their complexity, awesome in their vision, incredible in their detail. With a final click, the screen changes again, and there, surrounded by a thousand connections, you see your name at the centre of the screen. Your name, and the work you do. God says, 'With you, all this is possible.' And in a flash you see the history of the universe unfold, until eternity itself breaks into time and all is well.

Our work is part of God's redemptive purpose for the world. Or at least it can be, if submitted to God the Father as part of his desire to use us for the redeeming of humanity and the world.

Without this 'big picture' view, we will always be tempted to see work as a necessary evil, or somehow frowned upon by the church. In reality it is our primary place of ministry, and living out that ministry will affect those around us. For some of us it will affect people we will never meet. Our work can be part of God's redemptive plan for our world. It's that important.

Live by kingdom values

The thrust of this book is about exploring our faith with others, so the remainder of this chapter will focus on how we best do that in the workplace. To explore this I want to take us to Colossians 3. Here Paul gives some guidelines for living in a godly way which create the right context for the verses we've looked at so far about speaking of our faith.

Paul invites us to live as people of another kingdom, the kingdom of God. How do we do this?

Keep a right perspective (Colossians 3:1—4)

Setting out his guidelines for godly living, Paul urges us to remember the reality of what has happened to us, and to live by that reality now. Remember who you are: you have been raised with Christ. Remember where you are going: glory. Keep this perspective on all of life, including work, for work is not our god—God is. Amidst all the pressures these days, it is all too easy to let work become the centre of our lives. It pushes out other priorities which ought to take precedence: God himself, our family and friends.

Rob Parsons reminds us in his pithy book *The Sixty Minute Father* (Hodder and Stoughton) that no one has said on their deathbed, 'I wish I'd spent more time at the office.' Destroyed marriages, damaged children, distraught friends and a disappointed God litter the sidewalk of life as we allow work to rush us along routes we never intended to travel. We need to keep a right perspective. It is not easy. That's why God says so much about keeping a right perspective on his world and his work.

Die to wrong practices (Colossians 3:5—11)

'Put to death, therefore...' (v. 5). This is an act of the will. The tense of the verb is the present continuous, as Paul recognizes that it is not a once-in-a-lifetime decision but a daily decision to die to these things. They are no longer to live in our lives. 'Sexual immorality and impurity' (v. 5)—the temptation to think of colleagues inappropriately, to engage in inappropriate activity. 'Lust' (v. 5)—not just sexual, but the lust for power, position or popularity at the expense of character, integrity and other people. 'Evil desires and greed' (v. 5)—a longing to see someone get it wrong, a lifestyle which is no different from anyone else's, a credit card statement which doesn't reflect the priorities of the kingdom. 'Anger and rage' (v. 8)—the explosion at the ineptitude of others which devastates, even destroys people. How good are we at handling our anger? 'Slander and filthy language' (v. 8)—if every conversation about our colleagues was taped, would we be prepared for them to hear the recording? 'Lies' (v. 9)—the deceptive talk which promises more than we know we can deliver. The slippery talk which subtly shifts the blame away from where it rightfully resides—with us. Die to these practices, says Paul.

Develop right priorities (Colossians 3:12—4:1)

Again Paul starts with 'Therefore...' He means, *in the light of* putting to death these things, *in the light of* remembering who you are, 'God's chosen people, holy and dearly loved, *clothe yourselves...*' (v. 12).

The image is powerful. Just as we get up in the morning and put on clothes to prepare and protect ourselves for the day ahead, we are to clothe our inner self with these things.

'Compassion' (v. 12)—literally, to suffer with people. For me, compassion means constantly reminding myself that people come before projects, that my project goals need to be set aside if people are suffering. I don't find that easy, but I know it is a right priority.

'Kindness' (v. 12)—small acts are more significant than generous gestures. 'Humility' (v. 12)—the one we follow washed his colleagues' feet. How do we serve those we work with? 'Gentleness and patience' (v. 12)—not well known in many workplaces. Who is going to introduce them as ways of respecting people as people? 'Forgive grievances' (v. 13)—harbouring a grudge, biding your time, plotting revenge, are not options open to us. 'Love' (v. 14)—even your enemies.

How? How do we die to one list and come alive to the other? 'Let the peace of Christ rule in your hearts' and 'Let the word of Christ dwell in you richly,' says Paul (vv. 15–16). The process of change is one of transformation, not reformation. Jesus brings this about in us, we don't manufacture it within ourselves. What he requires is a willingness to be formed in his image, and a submission of our lives to his life.

This teaching is given to those who are members of the body of Christ. We are responsible for helping each other to live like this. Paul calls for us to be different, and to make a difference in our daily life.

Do it all for God

'Whatever you do, whether in word or deed, do it all in the name of the Lord Jesus, giving thanks to God the Father through him' (v. 17). We don't do our work primarily to get a wage packet, we don't do our work primarily for our boss. We are called to do our work to please Christ, and to do it in a way which will bring Christ to others. We work to further Christ's redemptive purposes in his world. This is our ministry.

Excellence in the workplace is a witness in itself—doing the best we can with what we have to honour Christ. Shirking our

responsibilities—because we're always at the coffee machine talking to others about Jesus—is not a good witness. Not only is the quality of our work important but also the spirit in which we do it. Imagine Jesus is our boss—now, how do we want to do our work?

Employee relations

Paul concludes this section of Colossians 3 with some words about our relationships. He calls us to have a proper attitude to those in authority (v. 22). We may want to say to Paul, 'You don't know my boss. You have no idea the moods he gets in, how unfairly he treats people.' Some of those whom Paul wrote to were slaves. I imagine they would have known something of the reality of unfair and unkind bosses, yet Paul reminds them to have a proper attitude to those in authority. Not grudging acquiescence or insincere lip-service, but a willingness to honour even the unreasonable, and to fulfil one's responsibilities well. 'It is the Lord Christ you are serving' (v. 24). Paul is not so blind as to ignore the wrong that may be done by bosses. We can stand up to injustice in the workplace, we can question inappropriate practice, we may even leave our work, but as long as we work for someone, we need to find a way of maintaining an appropriate attitude towards them.

He also calls for a proper attitude towards those who work for us: treat them fairly and with justice. How do we treat people for whom we are responsible? Do they see fairness and justice? Do we recognize the bigger picture of their lives outside the workplace and their personal needs? How are we enriching their lives through the work we're asking them to do? I read recently of the US ice-cream makers Ben and Jerry. In their three factories they pay everyone, from the Chief Executive to the packers, the same wage—and it's a good one. They even employ five people whose job is to make work fun for all the employees. Extreme. Unrealistic. Maybe, but it's visionary, radical, and very kingdom-like.

Keeping a right perspective, dying to wrong practices, developing right priorities, are a part of our witness in the workplace. Without these, we will run the risk of destroying the credibility of what we say.

A painful experience

When I was an idealistic and impressionable teenager, I went to work in a factory, sweeping floors and painting girders. The company was owned by a respected churchgoer in the community. He was as kind and generous to me as I could have wished, yet when I mentioned this to other employees they either exchanged knowing glances or muttered, 'You wait.' I didn't understand what was going on, until, that is, one Tuesday morning.

I was walking from one part of the factory to the other when I heard someone shouting. Rounding a corner, I found a small group of men standing beside a piece of machinery. In the middle was the company owner. I have never heard such foul language, seen such rage, witnessed someone so ruthlessly shredding every last bit of self-respect those men had. Something died inside me. I no longer respected the boss. Now I understood the mutterings of the men and women working in that place. They no longer respected the boss either. Even worse, they no longer respected Christianity.

We won't always get it right. We will make mistakes, lose our cool, treat people badly, but will we say sorry, will we allow Christ to change us, will we be honest and seek help? These are the marks of a follower of Jesus Christ. They will be a part of our witness.

When we apply these principles for living in 'kingdom ways', we shape the atmosphere and environment of the workplace. People recognize there is 'something about us'. They may not always be quick to mention it, but they watch, and one day they may want to speak about their life and possibly the faith. That's when we need to be ready to talk about our faith in a relaxed, natural and helpful way.

Talking about faith at work

What in particular can we do in the workplace when it comes to talking about our faith? The whole of this book is trying to help with this issue. We've identified the priority of prayer, the importance of being wise in the way we act towards outsiders, and making the most of every opportunity. We've explored ways to speak about our faith and handle common questions. All these things will apply in our workplace. Mark Greene, in an article in the *Church of England Newspaper*, suggested six specific aspects of evangelism in the workplace, which I've adapted.

Recognize that God is there before you

My friend Barry struggled to behave as he wanted at work. He thought he had to take God into work with him. In reality, God is already there before we arrive. If we are the only Christian in our place of work, the temptation is to think it is all up to us. It isn't. It is all up to God. God is at work in the lives of those around us, and he asks us to co-operate with what he is already doing. Barry and I prayed together before he went back into work. I suggested he prayed each day as he entered the building. 'Thank you, God, that you are here. Please help me to serve you well today.' It was a small beginning, but a radical step.

Realize that your very presence is a witness

By being a Christian in the workplace you are having an effect, and for the majority of time that will be a positive effect on those you work with. Whenever friends of mine say they are thinking of leaving their job to go into 'full-time Christian work', there's a part of me which sinks inside. It is tough being a Christian in the workplace, yet we need Christians who will act as salt and light in every area of work. Your work is your ministry. It *is* full-time Christian work. If you are in that position, please don't underestimate the effect of your presence.

Meet with others in similar situations

For some time I've been meeting a group of Christians who work in an office building near to my own place of work. They use one of our meeting rooms to pray once a week. A year ago, they didn't even know that each other existed. Some of them thought they were the only Christian in their building. Five hundred employees and they thought they were the only Christian. Talk about the odds stacked against you. Then, one of them took courage and circulated an e-mail. 'Anyone else out there?' Nine people responded. They now meet to encourage and help each other. If one of them is facing a particular difficulty, they e-mail the others. They pray together, talk about the issues they face, and look for opportunities to chat about their faith.

It's worth taking the plunge. Be brave. Find out if there are others in your place of work. If there are, meet with them, suggest how you could support one another, be honest about the real struggles. Why not work out together how best to talk about faith in your workplace?

The group meeting to pray in our building have recognized that they all commute from a wide geographical area. If their colleagues show any interest in Christianity, inviting them to their local church event or Alpha course is not always a viable option. It may mean a round trip of over one hundred miles. So we're talking about setting up an Alpha course at their place of work. Similar schemes have worked well elsewhere. Work is the place of their main contacts with people who aren't yet Christians. Work may well be the place to take those contacts on the next stage of their journey to faith.

If you are literally the only Christian in your workplace, either try finding others in the surrounding buildings, or meet with others in your local church. There are a number of good resources around to help you think through work issues. I've listed some at the end of the book.

Ask your minister to teach on work

If your minister doesn't feel able to do it, and no one in your church can, ask if you can invite in a Christian organization like Work Net that specializes in running workshops on workplace issues. Such teaching can encourage and equip us for the reality of daily life at work.

Learn to talk about a range of issues from a Christian perspective

This is hard work. Two friends I know agreed to help each other out. They decided to buy the same newspaper each day. Whatever the headline, they arranged to call each other at the start of their lunch-break to work out how to talk about that headline from a Christian perspective. After a year they had mastered the art. Their lunch-break conversations with colleagues were often fascinating conversations about topical issues and occasionally it led to opportunities to talk about their faith. There are everyday issues. There are personal issues affecting people's lives. There are work issues. All these can be approached with a Christian perspective.

Talk about your faith

The workplace is not meant to be a no-go area for your faith. Many hold back because they know that the witness of their lives doesn't back up what they want to say. Some hold back for fear of being made fun of, becoming the butt of every joke. Some hold back for fear of abusing a position of authority. Some hold back because they fear being seen as a soft touch. Whatever your reason, ask God to help you, talk to other Christians, and then pray for opportunities to share the faith. When they come, be sensitive to the fact that others may be listening in. Recognize that you may need to arrange a time and place to talk further so that you don't use up work time. Be aware of how your interest may be perceived, but don't hold back. Too much is at stake.

God is at work

Injit knows that the workplace can be a fairly hostile environment in which to be a Christian. Yet it's where he spends most of his time and it's where he has daily contact with those who aren't yet Christians. In Colossians, Paul suggests practical steps that Injit can take to further the work of Christ in his workplace.

Wherever we are 'at work', let's recognize it as a vital part of the church's ministry. Whatever the difficulties we face, let's try to find ways to talk openly about them with other Christians. However hard we find it, let's remember, God is at work—literally.

To consider

What are your greatest struggles as a Christian in the workplace? How could you find support and help with these? How might you best organize support for those in your church who are working?

A prayer
God of creation,
I offer you my work
and those I work with.
Help me to live by your priorities,
to work as if it was for you,
and to see you, Father, at work. Amen

Sunday: Mary, in bed

Mary rolled over in bed and stole a look at the alarm clock. 6.15 am. Another fifteen minutes.

The events of the previous evening continued to meander through her sleepy thoughts. All the family had come together for her dad's seventieth birthday: Shona travelled down from Birkenhead, Nick up from London. Dad's brothers and sisters had made it and, along with all the grandchildren, it was quite a gathering. Even Dad's dad had managed half an hour. Not bad at ninety-eight.

Bob stirred beside her.

It was a struggle being the only Christian. Shona showed interest, Nick just avoided the subject. Her parents were pleased that it helped her. Bob was supportive but sceptical. Benjamin, Joshua and Rebecca all came to church with her, but for how much longer?

'Naomi's preaching on evangelism again this morning,' she thought. 'Last week was good, but I wish I could talk to someone about my family situation. I don't seem to be getting anywhere.'

'Mummy,' whispered a little voice. Mary opened her eyes. Rebecca's face was inches away. 6.45 am. Not bad, an extra thirty minutes. Bob reached over and kissed Mary on the shoulder and ruffled Rebecca's hair.

'Good morning, all.'

Mary hoped it would be.

Chapter 9

Family matters

Whom do we find it most difficult to share our faith with? As I mentioned earlier, in my experience 'friends and family' is a common response. Mary is in that position. Her husband Bob doesn't mind that she is a Christian, except when it interferes with family outings on Sundays. Her children enjoy the children's activities at church. But she feels uncomfortable, even alone at times and, like many others in her situation, longs for Bob to become a Christian.

Some people are in worse situations. Their families actively make life difficult: snide comments, verbal abuse; for some, physical violence and being cut off from the family.

Why do many of us find 'family and friends' among the hardest people with whom to talk about our faith? What can Mary do about her situation?

Family and friends

I mentioned earlier in the book that Jesus himself had problems with his family and close friends. Let's take a closer look at two passages. In Mark 3:20–35, his family are concerned for his mental state. In Mark 6:1–6, Jesus is in his home town, and doesn't receive a favourable reception from those who know him well. Why do family and friends react like this?

They question our sense

'He is out of his mind' (Mark 3:21). His family wanted to take charge of him. With Jesus claiming to be God on earth, that is something of an understandable reaction, but sometimes our parents react almost as strongly when we commit ourselves to following Jesus. Some are deeply concerned about this 'new thing' their child has got involved in. Is it a cult? Is he or she being brainwashed? Others are angry that a child should choose something they have deliberately rejected. But the majority take the line, 'That's fine if it helps you, just don't push it on us.'

They know us well

'"Where did this man get these things? ... Isn't this the carpenter?" ... And they took offence at him' (Mark 6:2–3). Sometimes the disbelief is because they know what we are really like and cannot believe we have changed. Sometimes it's because we are most ourselves amongst our family. The masks we wear at church and among our Christian friends are stripped away as we enter the front door. Those closest to us know exactly what we can be like. Those who outwardly accept us silently question the genuineness of our faith. Those who are angry throw words at us which cut to the core: 'Call yourself a Christian?' Those who feel slighted by our enthusiasm, who have regarded themselves as Christians, resent the implications of our new-found faith.

'Jesus said to them, "Only in his home town, among his relatives and in his own house is a prophet without honour." He could not do any miracles there, except lay his hands on a few sick people and heal them. And he was amazed at their lack of faith' (Mark 6:4–6). You can feel Jesus' disappointment. This was one place where he may have expected to be 'at home' and instead he felt 'cast out'.

The anguish of the unknown

We care about our families. I received a letter from a friend. It described the last few months of her mother's life, who unexpectedly died of breast cancer. Miriam nursed her in the final weeks. She is full of grief. She writes, 'One of the saddest things is,

I don't know whether my mother turned to Jesus in the last hours of her life.' To modern minds this seems an extraordinary statement. To the mind formed by Jesus' perspective on life beyond death, this is the most anguishing of unknowns.

The possibility of eternity spent with God is something to shout from the rooftops. Eternity to be spent without God is too horrifying to contemplate. Most of us don't. Most of us avoid it. Jesus didn't. Not because he was some sadistic scaremonger, but because he knew the reality of being without God, in life and death. Eternity doesn't start when we die. Eternity starts when we accept Jesus as our rescuer, leader and friend. It starts now. If we know the reality of new life, we'll long for others to accept the one who gives it, especially those we love.

We've so much to lose. On the one hand we're anxious they may reject us. For some, that is a reality. I think of someone whose family is from another faith background. When he told them he had become a Christian, his father officially cut him off from the family: 'It will be as if you never existed.'

On the other hand we're anxious they may reject the faith. What if they say 'no', and continue to say 'no'? What if they say 'no' to their dying day? It is no use hiding behind glib platitudes: 'I'm sure they'll come to faith.' Some don't. That has to be possible if we believe that human beings have choice in the whole process of salvation. Where does that leave us? Do we even want to speak about the faith for fear of putting them off?

Heaven or hell?

People's eternal salvation is highlighted by the depth of concern and love we feel for our family. Part of me wishes I could say, 'Don't worry about hell. Everyone gets to heaven in the end, it will be all right.' But only part of me, for the consequences of a world where judgment doesn't exist are just as horrendous. A world where God said to Hitler, 'Six million Jews. Not good, but you're in anyway.' A world where God said to the Omagh bombers, 'Twenty-eight murdered. Not good, but you're in anyway.' A world where God said to the liar and cheat, 'You made it to the top through lying and cheating others. Not to worry, come on in.' A world where God said to the atheist, 'You chose not to believe in me, but bad luck, I exist, and you're with me for eternity.'

Thankfully, anyone can turn to God for forgiveness. And incredibly, God forgives—even Hitler—if we accept what he has done for us in Jesus. Yet if there is no judgment, our choices mean nothing. We could do whatever we wanted if we were all guaranteed a place in heaven. It would make a nonsense of God's character, because he is holy and therefore condemns all that is wrong. It would make a nonsense of our world, for ultimately might would be right, the strongest could do what they want and never fear being held accountable. It would make a nonsense of Jesus' mission on earth. What did he come to save us from?

God will hold us all accountable, yet I stress that not one person is beyond the reach of his forgiving love, however bad their actions. God doesn't send anyone to hell, we choose to go there. Jesus died to make it possible for us to receive forgiveness for all wrongdoing and assurance of life beyond death with God. We receive these things not because we are good, but because he is gracious. I long for everyone to receive this gift, especially those I love most, but they must choose and I must trust God—trust God that he does know what he is doing in his world even when I can't understand it.

With my family I have everything to lose, but I cannot hold back from sharing the faith with them because of that. For if I hold back, they have everything to lose, potentially for eternity.

When I was at university, I remember talking with a member of my wider family. We talked about Christian things. I longed for him to respond to Jesus, but I just wasn't getting through. Perhaps I was trying too hard. I started weeping. It was a combination of things. I loved him, I so longed for him to respond, I was so frustrated at my seeming inability to explain things clearly.

To be honest, I wish I wept a bit more for those I love. I'm sure Jesus does.

How do we share the faith with our families?

The danger is that the longing and loving sometimes lead to pressure being applied on those we love most. I've seen it done in all sorts of subtle and not so subtle ways. Everything from discreetly leaving Christian booklets round the house, to direct invitations to every evangelistic event within a hundred-mile radius. Pressure of any form is unlikely to be helpful, but there are some things we can do.

Let go

This is hard to do. In a subtle way, we may feel we are somehow responsible for their conversion. All the way through this book I have been trying to stress that God is responsible, not us. I found with my own family that I eventually reached the point of letting go. I picture in my mind's eye each member of my family who isn't a Christian and literally place them in the hands of God, trusting them to his care. I've seen some people do this who have been actively trying for twenty years to persuade their partners to become Christians. At first they think I've said something heretical. 'You mean I am not responsible?' they say. 'No, not ultimately,' I assure them. Their relief is tangible. I imagine their partners may discover some relief as well.

Continue to pray

After many years of praying, you may be wondering if there is anything new to say. This takes us back to Chapter 2, where we discussed ways to pray for those who aren't yet Christians. Be creative. For example, one member of my family lives abroad and I don't get to see him very often. When I do, I pray for opportunities, but invariably I muck them up. A few years ago I was over there and had three days alone with him. I was quietly praying for an opportunity and it came while we were fitting new lights in his kitchen. I missed it. Because of the distance I started to pray, 'Lord, would you bring across his path Christian people whom he gets to know, like, and respect.'

I was thrilled when my parents returned from visiting him a few months later to tell me that he had a new lodger—a committed Christian. That was some years ago. He's now married with no lodger, but I continue to pray for Christian people to cross his path.

We can also pray around the issues affecting people, be responsive to the situations they face and turn them into prayer. We can take the Bible and pray for its truths to become reality for the person. We can invite others to pray with us.

Introduce them to others

People come to faith normally through the influence and involvement of Christian people in their lives. If we're struggling to be that person for someone in our family, we can also introduce them to others who can play that role. Obviously we're not to manipulate situations and relationships, but if there are Christians who share the interests of the person in our family we're praying for, they may well get on and enjoy a developing friendship.

Last night, I had supper with some friends of mine. She had become a Christian while living with her then boyfriend. He eventually came to faith as well, and they had married. I asked him what most helped him on the journey. His response? 'Sharon's Christian friends. I imagined all Christians were weirdos in Jesus sandals. I discovered her new friends were normal, fun, and really committed to Jesus. In particular, one man helped—he enjoyed drinking red wine as much as I did. So we sat, drank and talked.'

Love them unconditionally

This is the toughest one of them all. Loving people is hard enough, but loving them unconditionally is incredibly hard, for genuine love has no strings attached. Unconditional love means we would love them no more if they became a Christian. Nagging and bullying do not lead people to Christ. They are expressions of conditional love. Let's take some time to reflect on our love for our family members. Are there ways our love is being warped by our desire for them to become Christians? Jesus is the only one who managed it perfectly, so let's not be too hard on ourselves. Ask him for help.

For the final section of this chapter, I want to focus briefly on three particular family relationships.

Parents

Respect is the key word. You may know Mark Twain's comment. As a fourteen-year-old he was appalled at his father's ignorance, and when he was twenty-one he commented, 'It's amazing how much my father has learnt in the last seven years.' We may think we know it all, but often our parents know a good deal more.

Respect any start they may have given you

You may not remember being baptized as an infant—they may never have taken you to church since—but on the day of your baptism you were prayed for. A congregation asked for God to be at work and bring you to faith in him. Your coming to faith is an answer to those prayers. They may have taught you some Christian values without introducing you to the value giver. Be thankful you don't have to completely overhaul your value system.

Respect their caution

They want to be sure you haven't hooked up with some weird group. If you're still a teenager, you may feel they are being overprotective. In fact, you may be an adult and feel that way. Respect their concern, and reassure them in any practical ways you can. Invite them to meet the minister, to come and see what it is like. Assure them of your love and concern for them.

Respect their need for time and space
This may be the most exciting and important thing that has ever happened to you, but it hasn't happened to them yet, so they don't see it quite like that. Parents often take a 'wait and see' attitude, particularly with their teenager's latest fad. Show them over the years that this isn't a passing trend, but a radical reorientation of your entire life.

Respect their advice
You may not agree with it, you may not take it, but respect it none the less. Listen carefully, talk honestly, and love consistently.

Respect opens the eyes and ears of parents more quickly than anything else. Respect honours them for who they are and what they have done for us. Respect acknowledges their unique position in our life, till their dying day. Respect is a commandment, after all: 'Honour your father and your mother' (Exodus 20:12).

Partners
Many unbelieving partners come to faith because of the example of their believing partner. I've heard the story again and again. 'He changed and I wanted to find out what caused the change.' 'She was different and although I was sceptical to start with, I couldn't help but be impressed.' In the home, the witness of a transformed life is powerful, but what if the partner doesn't come to faith, and is antagonistic to our faith? What do we do?

Keep the faith
That may sound obvious, but I've seen people who have lost their

faith through the attrition of an antagonistic partner. Jesus does talk about the priority of faith in him over even our closest family relationships. Only in extreme situations does it lead to separation on the grounds of faith, but Paul recognizes it as a possibility in 1 Corinthians 7:12–16.

Seek to understand the antagonism
If appropriate, we could ask our partner, 'Why do you feel like that? Why do you react in that way?' Let's not take such a conversation as an opportunity to put our point of view, simply try to listen and understand.

Avoid unnecessary irritation
Try not to leave Christian books and magazines all around the house. Avoid praying or reading the Bible when they are present. One woman I know gets up thirty minutes early to pray so as not to intrude on time with her partner. If we miss one Sunday at church to fit in with our partner's plans, it's not a disaster. Some believing partners don't make it to church on Sunday at all, but discipline themselves to go mid-week when it is more convenient for the family. Try not to spend every night out at a church-related activity.

Live in peace
Living in peace with our partner, behaving in a respectful and loving way, may well see the partner come to faith. Even if this, sadly, doesn't occur in our lifetime, we will have kept our faith in Jesus and the peace in our home. For the rest, all we can do is trust God.

Support one another
Listening to those in this situation, I've come to realize how incredibly difficult it can be. If you are able to find others in a similar position, support one another, and encourage your church to pray for you. It can be very tough.

Children

Our youngest child is two. He needs new shoes every eight to twelve weeks. It's alarming. Not for him, of course. For him, physical growth is the most natural thing on earth. The difficulty for us is keeping up with the speed of growth. Spiritually, children grow too. The pace often reflects the pace of physical growth, with different phases marked not by shoe size, but by faith stage. If we don't attend to their physical growth, their feet will soon be cramped, ultimately damaged. If we don't attend to their spiritual growth, the same occurs. When we go to the shoe shop the assistant measures their feet. Here are some markers for understanding the equivalent spiritual development of a child, taken from Gordon Bridgers' *Children Finding Faith* (Scripture Union).

Experienced faith

In the early years, babies and toddlers go where their parents go, do what their parents do, all the time absorbing their parents' likes, dislikes, values and interests. The importance of these younger years should not be underestimated. The child brought up in a Christian family is unlikely to question the existence of God at this stage, although they will be full of questions about the nature of God.

Affiliative faith

The child grows and other influences begin to play a major part in the formation of their world. School, friends and television dominate. At this stage, a child with a group of friends who go to church is unlikely to want to do anything else. Correspondingly, a much-liked teacher who openly rubbishes belief in God can have a devastating effect.

Searching faith

Through puberty and the turbulent teenage years, a child struggles with questions of self-identity, self-worth and self-understanding. Their capacity to move from concrete thinking to abstract thinking vastly increases. Things which were once accepted are now questioned and once-dearly held beliefs are all too easily rejected. Teenagers are searching for a faith which makes sense to them.

Owned faith
The faith of our parents and our friends is a great support, but at some point we have to determine to own that faith for ourselves. This adult decision may simply be another decision in a long line of decisions made throughout the child's life to continue to follow Jesus.

Human beings rarely fit a neat model of development. The model exists to help us understand stages of faith development but not as a prescription for how our child must develop. Some children own a real faith for themselves at a very young age. Some adults have not got to that point of ownership, or have delayed their searching stage till later in life. How we nurture faith in our children will depend on their age and stage of development, but I am absolutely convinced that at every age and every stage of life there is an appropriate relationship to be had with God. Spiritual development does not start at five, it begins at the moment of conception.

What can we do to nurture this development for babies and toddlers?

Model the priority of attending corporate worship
With two young children, I know what a hassle it can be getting along to church. For the last three years, one or other of us has sat in the crèche on a Sunday morning. Why bother to go? Why not stay at home in a warm environment with all their favourite toys on hand? Because a child learns what is important in life through the actions and activity of their parents. My two-year-old never

questions whether we will go to church on Sunday. He's done it all his life. He can't understand that other people *don't* go to church. The day will come when he will question it, but for now it is natural.

Model the priority of God in the home

What is distinctive about a Christian family? A desire to listen to what God has to say so that we can live in accordance with his will for our lives. Interacting with the Bible and prayer are two vital ways to enable that desire to become reality.

It helps to find appropriate ways to interact with the Bible with our children. We don't have to use some ancient dusty tome which is incomprehensible to us, let alone our two-year-old. There are plenty of excellent picture books which retell the Bible stories, and toddlers' and children's Bibles abound. There are also some great videos which retell Bible stories. My son's current favourite is a series called *Veggie Tales*. Superb computer animation combined with excellent music, captivating characterization and bags of humour make them addictive.

How about praying with and for our children? There is little more inspiring than hearing the prayers of a two-year-old as he talks with the creator of the universe, knowing that God hears every word and beams with love for this tiny child. If we're not used to praying out loud, we can buy a book of prayers to use with children and start there.

We can also pray with them as they experience the delights and difficulties of life. A friend told me how his daughter was enthralled with a beautiful sunset. They thanked God together. Another mentioned a recent occasion when she and her son witnessed an unpleasant accident. They prayed for those injured.

We can even introduce a family prayer time. Ours is after supper time and before bed time. It's brief and lively. We light some candles, sing some songs, read the Bible, talk about our day and concerns, pray individually and finish with the Lord's Prayer and a puff of smoke as two enthusiastic youngsters scrabble to be the first to blow out the candles. My colleague Stephen Cottrell has written more extensively about this in his book *Praying Through Life* (Church House Publishing, 1998).

Model the priority of God in our own life and homes
When children see us taking time to pray, to read our Bibles, to go to church, they learn. Allow them to join us once in a while and sit on our lap as we pray. Some of my most profound insights into God's character were early in the morning when our eldest didn't sleep so well. Struggling to pray, with William curled up contentedly on my lap, God taught me so much about his love for me.

Pre-school and infant school

Reflect what God is like
At this stage, reflecting the reality of what God is like becomes increasingly important. Before, the toddler couldn't articulate her faith, now the questions begin to fly. How we respond will act like a mirror to the child. The picture she sees in the mirror will become a lasting impression of the God she knows.

In parish ministry, I was involved in funerals. Disturbing and difficult times as they are, I was always deeply concerned for any child amongst the mourners. Phrases like 'God's taken Granny to be with him' seemed to slip out with ease from caring parents. We may have said it ourselves. Stop for a moment and think what such a phrase mirrors to the child about the nature of God. 'God's taken Granny away from me. I loved Granny. God's not very nice.'

Or here's another one. 'God's watching us and he sees everything we do. When we're good, God's very pleased with us, but when we are bad, he's cross and doesn't want us to do it again.' In the child's mind, God becomes an ogre figure in the sky to be feared and got rid of as soon as possible. In my work with adults, I come across so many people who are still living with an inaccurate and unhealthy image of God which was first 'mirrored' to them in their childhood.

Answer questions thoughtfully

We need to try to reflect God as he really is, to answer questions thoughtfully and sensitively, to explore issues with our children rather than telling them the answers, to listen carefully to their understanding and image of God so that we can provide gentle correction and helpful guidance.

Junior school

Manage their time

As the children become more and more independent, wanting to do their own thing, it helps to manage their use of time well. There are so many things they could be involved with. Are there ways we can help them to have a healthy balance of activities which meet their emotional, physical, mental *and* spiritual development?

In holidays, we could sign them up for a holiday Bible club, or offer to pay for them to go on a Christian activity holiday. So many children who have absorbed the faith from their parents come to embrace the faith for themselves at activities like this. They also discover that there are other young people who are Christians, and it introduces them to people who will be a role model for them of adult Christian living, crucial for those turbulent years that are just around the corner. During term time, it helps if we can continue to make time for prayer, interacting with the Bible and worship. If our church has an after-school club, we could encourage them to attend, even if it does mean missing some other activity.

Managing their time is not dictating exactly what they do, it's guiding them in ways which they'll enjoy and will lead to appropriate spiritual development.

Secondary school

Encourage questioning

This is when all the fun and hard work of the earlier years can pay off. As our children begin to question, doubt and debate the realities of what they have so far assumed to be true, they need to be given a safe context in which to be real about these issues. A child who feels he cannot question will flounder.

A friend of mine with two grown-up children put it like this:

Maturing faith in teenagers requires a mature response from us as adults. Questioning faith does not constitute a rejection of faith. Lying in on a Sunday morning and not coming to church does not mean the end of involvement. Being caught doing something previously unthought-of does not mean they've gone completely off the rails. They need to see in us a faith where words are matched by actions, where struggles are faced openly and honestly, where radical, idealistic initiative is embraced with loving, guiding hands, where mistakes are forgiven, and where security in God allows for freedom in life. At this stage we need to fit in with their agendas, be prepared to talk at two in the morning when they want to talk, accept we'll lose a few battles in order to win the campaign.

I've no experience of this stage, and I'm sure it won't be easy. But my friend's advice sounds good, even if I know it will be hard.

Children finding faith—adults finding faith

Key to all these approaches is a willingness throughout our lives to learn from our children. Faith development does not stop when you're an adult, it continues to our dying day, and children will be one of our greatest sources of instruction. Jesus said, 'I tell you the truth, anyone who will not receive the kingdom of God like a little child will never enter it' (Mark 10:15).

Family matters

Mary was finding her family difficult. So did Jesus. So may we. But just as they matter to us, they also matter to God. Our concern for them is more than matched by his concern for them.

Mary longs to talk openly about her family situation. My experience is that plenty of our churches have people who long to talk as well. Let's try to create places where that can happen, and let's support those, like Mary, who long to see those closest to them share the faith.

To consider

If we have close family who aren't yet Christians, what one thing could we do that would relieve any tension that may be present? How can we continue to pray for them in a creative way?

If we know of others who, like Mary, are finding their situation difficult, how can we best support them?

A prayer
Into your hands, O Lord,
I commit those I love
  [Take a moment to name them]

Take them,
and draw them to yourself. Amen

Sunday: back at church

'Let's pray.'

As she bows her head, Mrs Cray smiles at Injit—he's looking preoccupied. Geoff hopes that something Naomi says will help him with Nick and Pete at the pub. Mary still can't quite believe Bob said he would come on the church weekend away. Roger and Alison note that Naomi looks uncharacteristically nervous. Tom finishes his prayer for Rick to come to the Alpha course. Simon closes his eyes, regretting the all-night fishing.

After her prayer, Naomi looks up and shuffles from foot to foot. 'This is the second sermon in our series on evangelism. We'll be thinking about the passage from 2 Corinthians 5 in just a moment, but before I go any further I have an apology to make. A number of you spoke to me after last week's sermon. Tom in particular has helped me to see that what I said may have been less than helpful. I've asked him to come up and tell you what he said to me. Tom...'

Alison whispers to Roger, 'I wonder what they will make of this?' as Tom makes his way to the front.

'Thank you, Naomi. I spoke to Dorothy after the service last Sunday and she made me think. I decided to raise the whole issue of evangelism at the home-group on Wednesday night. Dorothy told us her feelings and struggles and it was like the floodgates opened. It seems we are all struggling with evangelism, so I thought I'd mention it to Naomi.

'Her sermon last week challenged a lot of us, I know, but in our home-group we wondered if Naomi's enthusiasm for

the subject, and her obvious evangelistic gifts, meant she didn't quite understand where most of us are at with evangelism. I told Naomi about the daily situations we identified in our home-group. They agreed I can tell you as well. We've all got things we're struggling with.

'Dorothy is trying to work out how to pray for people. Roger always seems to say the wrong thing in the office. Geoff wants to know how to make the most of opportunities that come up among his pigeon club friends. Alison—well, you know what has happened, and she wonders what she can say about her faith at this time. I've been talking to a friend at squash, but find it hard to be clear about what I believe. Simon fears being asked the difficult questions. Injit is snowed under at work and unsure how to witness in the workplace. Mary is really concerned about Bob, and would love to talk with someone in a similar situation. Maybe we are the only ones struggling, but we thought we needed to tell Naomi.'

Tom pauses and turns to look at Naomi.

'Naomi, we're struggling and we need some help.'

Tom returns to his seat. Alison reaches out a hand as he passes and whispers, 'Thank you.'

Chapter 10

The best-kept secret

It took some courage for Tom to say all that. It possibly took even more courage for Naomi to allow it to be said. She could easily have kept it quiet.

These questions and concerns are not unusual. What, in my experience, is unusual is to find a place in church where such issues can be faced honestly. Each of them is likely to undermine people's ability to talk about their faith with others. Evangelism is hard work, but it is made even harder when we can't tackle the internal and external issues which demotivate us from playing our part.

Back to our own stories

It would be so much easier not to bother, to leave it up to the experts like Naomi. Yet if we do, the church will decline. Why? To answer that question, let's go back to our own stories. How many of us, as we think back to how we came to faith in Christ, can identify a significant person or persons who helped us along the way? It may have been a mother or father who showed us what real faith looked like. It may have been a brother or sister who took us along to Sunday school. It may have been a friend, colleague, neighbour, acquaintance, minister, or youth leader. Was there someone for you who was significant? Someone God has written into your own story?

Whenever I ask that question of church groups, nearly everyone puts up their hand. I then invite them to call out the names of the people they have identified. The vast majority are completely unknown to the rest of us. Occasionally there is a well-known evangelist or minister in there, but the majority of the 'significant people' are unknowns—that is, unknown to us but not, of course, to God. For God chose to write these people into the stories of our lives just as he longs to write us into the stories of other people's lives.

He longs to take ordinary Christian people like us, and to use us to help other people come to know him, so that one day they will be telling their story and our name will be central to what they say. 'It was when I met Injit... I had this neighbour called Dorothy... Alison used to work with me... A squash partner called Tom invited me along to Alpha... We were both made redundant at the same time, Simon was his name... Geoff and I raced pigeons... Roger was my boss...' It could be our name, too.

How can we help each other?

If I am honest, I find it hard to keep focused and motivated to talk to others about my faith—and I am an evangelist! In my work life I am fortunate to have lots of opportunities to talk about Jesus with others, but if I am not living this out in my personal life it feels rather hollow. Praying for people I am in contact with in everyday life, making time to be with people who aren't yet Christians, taking the opportunities God gives me to speak of him and nurturing faith in my children are all priorities I believe in—passionately. But how easy it is not to live them out.

Two things have helped me. These aren't guarantees of success. I wish it was that easy—do this and you'll never have a problem with evangelism again. It just doesn't work like that, at least it doesn't for me. These are signposts which help to keep us travelling in the right direction. They have helped me and many others I know. Try them and see how they work for you. They are reflecting on the Bible and the support of other Christians.

Reflecting on the Bible

I am constantly challenged as I read the Bible. From beginning to end, it speaks of a God who longs for relationship with the people he has made. It reminds us of his pain at our separation from him. It humbles us with the knowledge of the extent to which his love is prepared to go, to restore our relationship with him. It inspires us with a vision of what is to come.

I mentioned at the start of this book that motivation for evangelism can only come from within. Something, or maybe more accurately someone, has to so grip us that we are inspired, challenged, and motivated to talk to others. As we reflect on the Bible—hear again God's story of his dealings with the world, regain God's perspective on life, feel God's passion for a world astray—we are changed and we begin to desire to play our part in God's work of drawing people to himself.

Reflecting on God's word leads to change in God's people and hope for God's world. Let me use 2 Corinthians 5 as an example. In this passage Paul speaks about a 'ministry of reconciliation' and mentions some things that keep him motivated in the face of persecution and hardship.

Paul was motivated by Christ's love

The pivotal verse for this section is verse 14: 'For Christ's love compels us.' Evangelism is not meant to be a dry duty or an additional activity, but an overflow of the love of Christ through us to others. I was sitting at the table the other day when my eldest son filled my glass up to the very brim. There was no way I could pick it up without it spilling. The merest nudge and water flowed. When we are so full of the love of Christ, people will only have to bump into us and it will overflow. His love is compelling love, it motivates us to action, it inspires us to care, it unites us in a common vision. How do we fill up with this love of Christ? There are many ways, but Paul draws our attention to one: by meditating on Christ's sacrifice.

Paul was motivated by the reality of Christ's sacrifice

Paul is convinced that 'one died for all and therefore all died' (v. 14). Just as his heart is filled with the love of Christ, his mind is filled with the truth about Christ's sacrifice. He died for all. His death is not just for those of us who have accepted what he achieved for us on the cross, it's for everyone. Paul was so convinced of this that he was prepared to stick at it, whatever happenend to him. When we face struggles, something has to grip us, in our heart and in our head, to help us through.

I find it really helpful to read the accounts of Jesus' crucifixion, to read them slowly, and after each verse pause and say to myself, 'He did this for me.' Often I am in tears as I am overwhelmed with the love of Christ for me. More recently, I've started adding, 'He did it for...' and I name someone I know who isn't yet a Christian. The reality of this seeps into my mind, and convinces me of the truth. Jesus' sacrifice was for me, and for all those I know. Paul kept going because he meditated on the cross.

Paul was motivated by Christ's perspective

Paul continues, 'So from now on we regard no one from a worldly point of view' (v. 16). Christ's perspective motivated Paul to see people differently. It's so easy to dismiss people, but Paul doesn't write anybody off. Rather, he sees them through Jesus' eyes. Whom do we easily dismiss?

No one is to be dismissed, no one is excluded from Christ's sacrifice, no one is beyond his reach. Yet I sometimes think to myself, 'Sam's life is going well. He's got everything he needs, good job, nice car, great family, and he's really happy with life. He's not going to be interested in Christianity.' It's a terrible attitude, and I know I need Christ's perspective to transform the way I look at people and situations. From Christ's perspective, Sam is without the most important thing in life, a right relationship with God.

Christ's perspective kept Paul open to all the opportunities he had to speak about his faith with others.

Paul was motivated by Christ's power

In verse 17, Paul says, 'Therefore, if anyone is in Christ he is a new creation; the old has gone, the new has come!' This has to be the greatest miracle of all—a new creation, a new life, and a new future. The same power which brought the world into being is focused on an individual and transforms their world. Here is another way I try to maintain motivation—I reflect on what it means for me to be a new creation. I find it all too easy to take it for granted. As I thank God for what he has done in my life, and his power to change me, I find it increases my longing for him to do that in the lives of others.

Paul was motivated by Christ's call

Paul reflects on this 'ministry of reconciliation' given to him by God. Note that Paul recognizes, 'All this is from God' (v. 18). God is the initiator in evangelism. If we stop believing that, we'll quickly become demotivated because we'll feel the responsibility too acutely.

Paul knows that Jesus brought about the reconciliation. He states as much in verse 18. His part was to be an ambassador (v. 20), the one through whom God makes his appeal. An ambassador is responsible for promoting the best interests of the kingdom he or she represents in foreign parts. The kingdom we belong to is not of this world. As Christians, we are called to be ambassadors of that kingdom, representing the King in foreign parts. This is part of our calling.

Paul was motivated by the body of Christ

Ambassadors don't work on their own. They go out from the embassy to fulfil their duties, but they return to the embassy for support. Throughout this passage, Paul speaks in the first person plural—'we'. What helped him keep on going? The reality of being part of the body of Christ—that this ministry was a shared one, one in which he had a part to play, but not on his own. Nor are we on our own. Or at least we shouldn't be. Church life is meant to help us to live the Christian life.

The support of other Christians

Reflecting on the Bible really helps me to keep motivated, but I know how easy it is to be full of good intentions and not do anything about them. The second thing that helps me to keep focused on evangelism is the support of other Christians.

Encourage one another

The word 'encourage' has become something of a cliché in many Christian circles, but it is a good word. It means 'to give strength to' That's certainly what I need—people who will give strength to me. Because evangelism is not easy, I need constant support and help to keep on with it. How can a church do that?

Focus one another on evangelism

If the whole church sees evangelism as a central part of its ministry, then it is a lot easier for me as an individual to play my part. Some of us will be in churches like that, others will not. For five years of my Christian life, I attended a church which didn't have a strong concern for helping others come to faith. I survived, but I admit it wasn't easy. If we're in churches like that, we may be able sensitively to raise concerns about an evangelism focus. There are some excellent resources available to help us. I've listed some at the end of the book. If you are a minority within your church, some of the other suggestions may help you to keep going even if the church as a whole is not very supportive.

Equip one another for evangelism

Many of the issues identified by Tom's home-group are addressed in various training courses that exist to help people talk about their faith. This book has its origins in a course called *Lost for Words*. Actually meeting with people and working through some material together can be immensely helpful, as we gain insights and ideas from one another. I know of churches that try to run such a course on a regular basis, because it becomes appropriate for different people at different times. They also have new people joining the church, so the course both shows one of the priorities in the life of the church and provides a practical way of helping new people discover their part in evangelism.

Hold one another accountable

I don't mean by this a heavy-handed checking up on people; rather, helping people to do what they want to do. I want to pray for people I know who aren't Christians, but it is so easy to forget or let it slip. What keeps me praying? Knowing that I am going to meet with other Christians who are going to ask me how my praying is going.

For some of us, our home-group could fulfil that function. Each time we meet, we could take time to talk about how we are getting on with evangelism. Not in a guilt-inducing, finger-pointing, condemning way, but in a mutually supportive, encouraging way.

For some, other meetings with Christians could provide the opportunity for this sort of accountability. It may be a formal meeting such as a church leadership team, or a more informal one with a friend over coffee. If you have no place for such accountability, how about seeking out one or two other Christians who you think may be open to meeting for mutual support and help with evangelism. Some churches have called these 'prayer triplets'. You may have to take the initiative but, if successful, it will be worth it.

A way forward

Here are two possible ways to help one another with evangelism: reflecting on the Bible so that our perspectives on life are constantly refined to be more in line with God's, and supporting one another so that we do what we intend to do. I commend them. The good news is too good to keep to ourselves.

A best-kept secret

The Australian comedian Paul Hogan is best known for his role in the *Crocodile Dundee* films. He's made a less well-known film called *Almost an Angel*. In it he plays the part of Jack, a crook who is coming out of jail for the umpteenth time. He's walking along the sidewalk when he sees a little boy kick his football into the road. The boy chases after the ball, oblivious to the juggernaut trundling his way. For once, Jack does something right in his life. He leaps into the road, pushes the boy aside, and in the process is crushed by the wheels of the juggernaut. He dies and wakes up in heaven. God turns up, looking remarkably like Charlton Heston. He looks at Jack and says, 'You scumbag.' Jack is a little shocked, first of all to discover that God exists and secondly that he speaks in this way. To cut a long story short, Jack gets sent back down to earth to make amends for his ways. He meets a man in a wheelchair and his sister, who provides the romantic interest for the film. There's a very telling scene. Jack's walking along beside the man in the wheelchair when he discovers the man knows a thing or two about God. Jack stops. He looks at him and says, 'Geesh, you Christians sure know how to keep a good secret.'

My prayer is that this book may go just a little way to helping us talk about the world's best-kept secret, so that we would no longer be 'lost for words'.

To consider

What would help you to keep motivated in talking about your faith?

To whom could you make yourself accountable for support and encouragement?

A prayer
Lord, here I am.
Use me. Amen

Resources

Richard Higginson, *Mind the Gap* (CPAS)

Mark Greene, *God on Monday* (SU)

Robert Warren, *Launching a Missionary Congregation* (CPAS)

Emmaus (Bible Society)

Leighton Ford, *The Power of Story* (NavPress)

Nick Pollard, *Evangelism Made Slightly Less Difficult* (IVP)

Justyn Rees, *Love Your Neighbour—For God's Sake* (Hodder)

John Chapman, *Know and Tell the Gospel* (St Matthias Press)

Richard Higginson, *Called to Account* (Eagle)

Rob Parsons, *The Sixty Minute Father* (Hodder and Stoughton)

Gordon Bridgers, *Children Finding Faith* (Scripture Union)

Stephen Cottrell, *Praying Through Life* (Church House Publishing)

Paul Morris, *Gearing Up for Mission* (CPAS)

Appendix: Lost for Words course

Lost for Words exists as a six-session course to use in your local church. Full of practical ideas, it provides an opportunity to address many of the issues covered in this book in a more 'hands-on' way.

This course is available from CPAS at the address below. Do contact us if you would like further details.

CPAS
Athena Drive
Tachbrook Park
Warwick
CV34 6NG

Tel: 01926 458458
Fax: 01926 458459